MW00323817

the americas

The Origin of Species
and Other Poems

Ernesto Cardenal

Translated and introduced by John Lyons

Foreword by Anne Waldman

Texas Tech University Press

"Ernesto Cardenal and I," by Roberto Bolaño, translated by Laura Healy. From
Romantic Dogs, copyright © 2006 by the Heirs of Roberto Bolaño. Translation
copyright © 2008 by Laura Healy. Reprinted by permission of New Directions
Publishing Corp. The poem also appeared in *Poetry* in November 2008.

This book is typeset in Monotype Fairfield. The paper used in this book meets the
minimum requirements of ANSI/NISO Z39.48-1992 (R1997). ∞

Library of Congress Cataloging-in-Publication Data
Cardenal, Ernesto.
   [Poems. English. Selections]
   The origin of species and other poems / Ernesto Cardenal ; translated and intro-
duced by John Lyons ; foreword by Anne Waldman.
      p. cm.—(The Americas)
   Includes bibliographical references.
   Summary: "Along with its title poem, a meditation on Charles Darwin's theory of
evolution, this volume by Latin American poet Ernesto Cardenal includes twenty
new poems—some appearing for the first time in English and some previously
unpublished—and new cantos supplementing Cosmic Canticle"—Provided by pub-
lisher.
   ISBN 978-0-89672-689-5 (hardcover : alk. paper)
1. Cardenal, Ernesto — Translations into English. I. Lyons, John. II. Title.
   PQ7519.C34A2 2011
   861'.64—dc22
                                                      2011000797

Printed in the United States of America

11 12 13 14 15 16 17 18 19 / 9 8 7 6 5 4 3 2 1

Texas Tech University Press | Box 41037 | Lubbock, Texas 79409-1037 USA
800.832.4042 | ttup@ttu.edu | www.ttup.ttu.edu | www.ttupress.org

CONTENTS

Foreword

Anne Waldman

Ernesto Cardenal is one of the world's most ethically astute and conscientious poets. As a Nicaraguan, writing in Spanish, personally caught up in the struggles of his country, his continent and his times, Cardenal has been a cultural icon whose long life of service in the cause of humanity is legendary. His attentiveness to the "minute particulars" of his own life and studies, to his travels and encounters, to his spiritual concerns and practices is extraordinarily rich and inspiring.

One is stimulated and enlarged by the mind of this poet, whose rigor of attention—his word, line, sound, image, perception, and thinking—raises the possibilities for poetry as a vehicle of radical transformation.

Everything *out there* is to be plumbed and explored. As he summons and notes details of landscape, species, poetic lore, we realize it is the phenomenal world that rouses his insatiable curiosity. His optimism is constantly radiating with a scholarly wonder. His clear-eyed empathy and philosophical meditation on life's mysteries is infectious. His ways and manners as he navigates these mysteries with devoted attention and consummate faith, traversing time and space, is at the core of his major new book, *The Origin of Species and Other Poems,* a book which commemorates Darwin's consciousness-altering treatise.

There is also deep pleasure intuiting Cardenal's essential humility. In these rapt narratives of cultural and social history, his meetings with dignitaries, and his friendships, his scrutinizing descriptions of place, from French prehistoric caves ("mysticism is prehistoric") to travels with the Lapps, to travels in Mexico and Germany, Cardenal is *not* at the center. In a particularly telling encounter, the poet travels with a copy of *The White Goddess,* which he has been assiduously studying and contemplating, to Robert Graves's door in Deyá, Majorca. This is his first trip to Europe; he has been reading Graves's book "on the sun-lounger on deck, / watching the wake / from the stern / —Poseidon's curly hair—." He is welcomed by the poet ("with unkempt graying hair /and in a country suit like one of those / gamekeepers in Engish novels") with a bowl of hot soup, and Graves shows his children Nicaragua on a small globe.

Cardenal shares a lineage with mystical thinkers from all times, whose spiritual faith guides their work. I use the word "spiritual" without hesitation, as contrasted with "religious." Cardenal does not keep piety with orthodoxy or institutionalized religion. He has said he considers religion harmful because it divides humanity. Anna Akhmatova, the Russian Orthodox Christian, and Denise Levertov of recent years, an activist who converted late to the Catholic faith, come to mind, as do T. S. Eliot and Wystan Auden, the latter who shares with Cardenal a love of the wry and charming detail. But Cardenal resonates often with the Whitman of the open road and the peripatetic ambassador of a Buddhist Beat ethos Allen Ginsberg, whose mentor on "tangibles" was William Carlos Williams and others of the Objectivist school that Cardenal admired. Cardenal, like these mentioned, is a citizen of the world. He also carries the lineages of his own America to the south and the rich legacy of numerous Mexican and Central and Latin American poets.

William Carlos Williams wrote that the job of the poet is to move the century forward a few inches. Cardenal holds a unique position in the annals of contemporary postmodern literature, having already accomplished this feat in *Cosmic Canticle,* an epic tome which includes a disturbing prescient prophecy of both 9/11 and the collapse of Wall Street. He soldiers on at the age of eighty-five with ever more rigorous and prodigious new writing.

Much of *The Origin of Species* is composed of a series of narrative investigatory poem-treatises or mini-essays; and as such offers a kind of guidebook through this poet's literal and mental terrains.

Cardenal actively participated in the Nicaraguan revolution, becoming the Minister of Culture of Nicaragua under the Sandinistas. He is a proponent of radical liberation theology and communal utopias, and writes simultaneously as an intellectual, a contemplative, and a social activist. He also follows quantum theory.

At a time when evolution and religion vie for clarity—in some minds, dominance—a position that would seem oxymoronic or logistically impossible, Cardenal moves the thinking forward here. He holds the both/and position. Whether one accepts Cardenal's basic premise of "all life on the earth coming from a single cell," and therefore "if one rises from the dead / we all rise from the dead," one feels provoked and stirred by the discourse, which is for many the most definitive and provocative discussion of our time. As scientists such as Stephen Hawking grapple with what he calls "M-Theory," clearly a secular view, and others ban and censor books on evolution in classrooms, Cardenal's stance is steady. It carries an informed yet mystical conviction. He is deeply absorbed—and motivated—by the tangible beauties and complexities of the natural world, and by a vision for the future that transcends nihilism or eternalism.

The poems of *The Origin of Species* are aptly translated by John Lyons, who keeps the flow and integrity of Cardenal's thought patterns and images moving forward with intelligence and grace. There is a summing-up here, in poems that cover an enormous swath of experience, travel, conversation, meditation, and *gnosis*—and perhaps a sense of urgency, as well. I remember Ernesto once saying in conversation that he wrote for young people of the future. This is not a sentimental project. It is instructional, true, balanced, sane.

The title poem conjures from the first—tracking Darwin's own logic and science—the mystery of island life, how finches in the Galápagos "with different beaks" differentiate according to their environment:

> *pincer-like beaks for insects*
> *sharp to perforate barks*
> *like tongs for harder seeds*
> > *the thicker seeds*
> > *thickened the beaks*

There Lyons has caught the urgency of the push of the species, the vivid life of the beaks that cut and chew, the sounds of the hard *b*, *k*, and *t*.

The evolutionary march continues:

> *and other creatures*
> *[. . .]*
> *"adapting to the environment"*
> *[. . .]*
> *fins of fish develop*
> *into paws of invertebrates*
> > *"we are all a modification of another"*

The evolution of the eye, "absurd," Darwin notes, from a "single photoelectric cell" is now "forty varieties of eye"! This is wondrous.

> > *"to evolve" means*
> > *to unroll a scroll*
> > *and we cannot change direction*

The scroll unrolls further in a delightful litany of our hybrid origins:

> *closer to the mushroom than to the carnation*
> *[. . .]*
> *and the beaks in the Galapagos change*
> *[. . .]*

Microscopic algae
now immense trees
[. . .]
women breastfeed like seals
[. . .]
the teeth with which I eat a lobster
are like those of the lobster

I find this last particularly arresting. A stunning Objectivist moment, as in Williams's "no ideas but in things," with an additional Whitmanesque lilt.

The litany of life builds further:
the spider with legs the color of air
beating upon its web of threads of air
Iguana with its chlorophyll camouflage
wild flower with its Paris perfume
string of silvery fish
    like a piece of the sea
aquatic flowers like ballet dancers
   the elastic cat asleep
    on the kitchen floor
the monkeys' vociferous hullabaloo
she known as Carmen in Granada
a small toad on a leaf

And soon we come to the crux of Cardenal's faith:

"God": imperfect conception
as the electron also is
without the electron being an illusion
The explanation of the Holocaust:
That to create he ceased to be God
Creation as kenosis (emptying
of God) impotent in the face of Pinochet
   And a God not anthropomorphic
   but one with whom I can talk

The notion that having first created our world, God ceased to be God is very Zen-like and is a question at the heart of Cardenal's logic, language, and thinking. He does not see this God as salvation necessarily, nor does he invoke Adorno's question about atrocity in the face of annihilation (i.e., the Holocaust). This notion of keno-sis—*of God making himself into nothing*—resembles a koan, a para-doxical riddle used in Zen Buddhist meditation to provoke insight or knowledge. It also presumes a kind of "negative capability," of being able to hold contradictions in the mind without "any irritable reach after fact or reason." It requires a certain faith to hold this in the mind and to explore the permutations and rationale for an acceptance of God.

The sixteenth-century Spanish mystical theologian St. John of the Cross held similar views, shown in Philippians 2:7 concerning how "Jesus made himself nothing," and how one might "self-empty one's will" toward God. It suggests that a sense of *pratitya-samutpada*—in Sanskrit, the co-arising and interconnectedness of all living things—prevails. Cardenal knows well the vicissitudes of injustice, poverty, struggle, and war. He knows the economic under-pinnings of degradation and oppression. He is also a visionary and benevolent socialist at heart. He refers twice to 1 Corinthians 15:17: "If He has not risen, we're fucked."

For Cardenal the world is not static. It is an open system, a dis-sipative structure. We are in a dance with entropy. As a result, he is able to also envision a stranger, perhaps cyborgian, future, as in "Manaus Revisited."

> technology is also biological
>   like carapace or shell
> our descendants could be made of silicon
>   or alloy

The book holds long narrative poems, including a particularly stirring tribute and meditation on Don Vasco de Quiroga, known affectionately as "Tata (Papa) Vasco" which is the title of this hagio-graphical piece. Quiroga came to Mexico through the auspices of Emperor Charles V. Having read Thomas More's *Utopia*, he tried to implement a similar enlightened system among the indigenous people—the Tarascans—of Michoacán. As anyone who visits this area knows, Tata Vasco remains an enshrined and endearing figure for his work in land and agricultural reform, as well as in the arts and handicrafts. His was a utopia that took care of the sick, orphans, widows, and elderly. "The people without jails. / Without death penalty."

As Cardenal writes:

> *Quiroga discovered the unknown man of Michoacán:*
> *the Artist.*

And among many notable accomplishments of Quiroga, he renders a detailed account of the lacquer-ware of Uruapan ("where the flowers open"), and how the pigment comes from the insect *aje*:

> *first the drawing with a knife*
> *the details next with a bodkin*
> *the colors rubbed in with the finger*
> *[. . .]*
> *lilies, pansies, daisies, violets, forget-me-nots*
> *every color of petal and green of the flower stems*
> *with black background and blue black, blue, yellow, red, cherry;*
> *colors of ajes crushed in oil which never fade*

The poem ends with the poet seeing the compassionate hand and intelligence of Vasco's vision everywhere. And he looks at Lake Pátzcuaro, as if for the last time:

> *White fish of Pátzcuaro*
> *The shining skin of silver and diamonds*
> *in garlic sauce*

It is these luminous details that continue to startle and animate the trajectory of this book.

I interviewed Ernesto Cardenal in 2001, right after the events of 9/11. After we had discussed the implications of the attack on the World Trade Center and the Shock and Awe campaign that was being waged in Afghanistan, I asked him how his faith sustained him "in these times." He replied:

I believe capitalism will end because it is an unjust system, and because the laws of evolution are about more and more union, more and more love among our species. Particles unite to form the atom, atoms unite to form the molecule, molecules unite to form the organism, organisms unite to form the society. And society, for some time now, tries to have less and less inequality. We overcame slavery and feudalism, and now it's time to overcome capitalism. Later on we'll surpass socialism too. Then we'll have a perfect system. In a poem of mine I say that communism and the Kingdom of Heaven are the same. This faith sustains me both as a Christian and a Revolutionary. I believe in God's reign, that is—equality—as well as I believe in the social revolution. The expression *Kingdom of Heaven* in Jesus's time meant exactly what the word *revolution* means now. It was equally subversive.

A compelling poem by the Chilean novelist and poet Roberto Bolaño, "Ernesto Cardenal and I," queries Cardenal's view "that communism and the Kingdom of Heaven are the same." Bolaño seems to be asking, if there is this unconditional love and acceptance from God—this "equality"—does it in any way lessen the chill of "botanical frigidity"? Does the natural world really care about the life and death or salvation of humanity? The further question is, can these two views co-exist?

Father, in the Kingdom of Heaven
that is communism,
is there a place for homosexuals?
Yes, he said.
And for impenitent masturbators?
For sex slaves?
For sex fools?
For sadomasochists, for whores, for those obsessed
with enemas,
for those who can't take it anymore, those who really truly
can't take it anymore?
And Cardenal said yes.
And I raised my eyes
and the clouds looked like
the pale pink smiles of cats
and the trees cross-stitched on the hill
(the hill we've got to climb)
shook their branches.
Savage trees, as if saying

some day, sooner rather than later, you'll have to come
into my rubbery arms, into my scraggly arms,
into my cold arms. A botanical frigidity
that'll stand your hair on end.

In the current collection, Cardenal's response is found in
"Reflections on the River Grijalva," an account of overlooking a
magnificent cañon in Chiapas, Mexico, as seen from a *mirador*, or
observation deck, "the best panorama in the world," and from a
launch along the river.

> *souvenirs and postcards in the snack bar*
> *the geological formation is*
> *at least 12 million years old*
> *touch the rock*

> *I watch the pelicans*
> > *as though on air command maneuvers*
> *[. . .]*
> *below the sheer cliffs*
> *flow the rapids and torrents*
> *into which the Chiapas Indians threw themselves*

The poet assumes a nihilist view:

> *the clear or dirty water of the Grijalva*
> > *what does it matter*
> *[. . .]*
> > *and all cosmic teleology*
> > *a psychological projection*
> > *in a meaningless universe*
> > *its evolution directionless*
> *the evolution of an eye not knowing what it will see!*

There's next an encounter with a "fetid carpet," much like the
"islands" or continents of detritus in the world's oceans, this one a
kilometer in length:

> *of detergents   coca-cola   ketchup   shampoos   Kellogg   Tabasco*
> *chile   bottles   plastic   bags   bags   bags   Colgate   toothpaste*

Gillette cream tires empty packaging Eau de Cologne open
cans Listerine box of Kleenex piece of shoe dead cat rags etc . . .

He continues:

> *Could the universe not care less*
> *about the ecological anxieties*
> *of just a few mad fools?*
> *Or does the universe cry out through us?*

And as the position shifts:

> *every entity is relationship*
> *relationship is the true substance of being*
> *and even the Trinity is relationship*
> *atoms aren't the same observed*
> *as not observed*
> *which is why we are not unnecessary in the cosmos*
> *But are we observers important*
> *with our lavish waste in this tiny corner?*
> *Who cares what's thrown into the Grijalva?*

Cardenal seems to think we *could* be bothered, and of course
the natural world *is* bothered. It is not indifferent to our environ-
mental degradation. There *is* the test of our humanity up against an
indifferent perspective which is our own indifference, a chill world
which could be us. We are also Bolaño's rubbery, scraggly trees.
There is always a relationship. And in the contest between eternal-
ism and nihilism, this is an important measure, it is humanity's
measure. We might see the trees as savage, as threatening, we
might imagine the slime molds inheriting the earth—and they have
a pretty good time of it as it is—but we can do the work of evolving
while we're here.

There is a heartening progressive ecology at work in Cardenal's
poetry, at every turn, towards the "more perfect union." It is a Whit-
manesque embrace and also a timely political and spiritual reso-
nance with a particularly difficult and early-broken-hearted new
century. And there is a pragmatism and surety at the same time. I
think of Gary Snyder's sense of the "wild" and of wilderness being
"without a management plan."

The practice of the wild in Snyder's sense inspires *an etiquette of freedom*. You take care of things because it is beautiful to do so. Cardenal has taken care in his poetic and spiritual practice of so much around him. He has been the complete, skillful witness. This book shines in what some would call the autumn of this poet's life. It is a rich and varied testimony of a full and varied life. Cardenal is never sentimental or frightened about death. As he writes in "White Holes" of his friend Rosario Castellanos and of their friendship 45 years ago, and of her death and then meeting her in a dream:

There is a mystery at the end of the universe
and you are now within it.
Unless we die others are not born.
And through the death of others we have been born.
Without death there'd be no human species
nor any species
[. . .]
Without death there'd be no future

These beautiful and instructive poems, and there are many more of them here in *The Origin of Species*, arrive finally as a kind of urgent intervention. And as the science-versus-spiritual debate continues, they offer a respite, an alternative, and a bigger view.

Infinite vastness of tiny conifers
of a sad green
in the melancholy light of dusk
    "With the Lapps"

"So his footprint would not be erased" is the concluding line in Cardenal's homage to Quiroga. May it also stand as a talismanic image for these shimmering poems.

Introduction

The Poetics of Contemplation

The title poem of this new collection[1] of poetry by Ernesto Carde-
nal, "The Origin of Species," was written to commemorate the
bicentenary of the birth of the naturalist Charles Darwin. Com-
posed in his eighty-fifth year, Cardenal's text is, by any standard, a
poetic *tour de force*, a truly remarkable reflection on the implica-
tions of Darwin's famous theory of evolution. In 1989, Curbstone
Press in Connecticut published Cardenal's *Cosmic Canticle*, a mas-
terly four-hundred-page meditation on the origins of the cosmos,
which began with the Big Bang and which has continued to evolve
since that critical moment:

> *In the beginning there was nothing*
> > *neither space*
> > *nor time.*
> > *The entire universe concentrated*
> *in the space of the nucleus of an atom,*
> *and before that even less, much less than a proton,*
> *and even less still, an infinitely dense mathematical point.*
> > *And that was Big Bang.*

Similarly, Cardenal's "The Origin of Species" opens with a sin-
gle, simple statement which sets the entire poetic sequence in
motion:

That all life on earth
should come from a single cell:
  *the great mystery*²

What Cardenal captures here is that that second critical
moment in the development of the cosmos, when energies coa-
lesced to produce a single biological cell that then proceeded to
divide and further divide in a process we call life, was an historical
event every bit as momentous as the Big Bang. This initial observa-
tion provides, in a sense, the DNA or genetic code for the entire
poem, which grows in detail or complexity as the accumulated
information and references unfold in a relentless, compelling
rhythm.

One of the major themes of *Cosmic Canticle* relates to the sec-
ond law of thermodynamics and entropy, manifest in the constant
deterioration of high-energy quanta into low-energy quanta: "energy
is indestructible in quantity / but continually changes in form." In
contrast to this, "The Origin of Species" emphasizes that biological
life, through a process of variation and natural selection, tends to
move in the direction of ever-increasing complexity, a crucial aspect
of which is the evolution of consciousness and the brain, "the cos-
mological miracle / of human presence in the cosmos."

If all species are interlinked because of their descent from a
common ancestor, Cardenal's proposal is that our destinies are also
interlinked:

Evolution unites us all
the living and the dead
Darwin discovered it
  (that we come from a single cell)
that is we are interlinked
  if one rises from the dead
  we all rise from the dead

And it is this leap of faith in the resurrection of the body that
distinguishes Cardenal's discourse from that of Darwin. His argu-
ment is that Darwin, who prior to becoming a naturalist had con-
sidered entering the Anglican priesthood, developed the theory of
the variability or division of species through natural selection,
which does not account, however, for the origin of life itself. Or to

put it in Cardenal's own words, Darwin "speaks of the modifica-
tions / of species not the origin / the origin is a mystery." What
came before the Big Bang? Why did life and human consciousness
appear in the cosmos? And what is the ultimate purpose of this evo-
lution? If these three questions are central to Cardenal's poetics, it
is useful to know a little about the poet's life.

Born in Nicaragua in 1925, Ernesto Cardenal, a frequent nomi-
nee for the Nobel Prize for Literature, is the most important poet
writing in Spanish today; and the appreciation of his poetry may be
enhanced by an understanding of two essential factors. The first
relates to Cardenal's religious vocation, which led him to enter a
monastery of the Order of Cistercians of the Strict Observance in
Kentucky in 1957, where he came under the influence of novice
master Thomas Merton, who at the time was an author internation-
ally renowned for his writings on current affairs and the contempla-
tive life. In fact, it was the presence of Merton that initially drew
Cardenal to Kentucky. Cardenal subsequently moved to a more lib-
eral Benedictine community based outside the Mexican city of
Cuernavaca in 1959, before entering La Ceja seminary in Colombia
in 1961, where he completed his studies for the priesthood. He was
ordained as a Roman Catholic priest in August 1965. On his return
to Nicaragua in that year, Cardenal established a contemplative
community on the island of Solentiname in the Great Lake of
Nicaragua where he ministered to the inhabitants of the surround-
ing islands. Encouraged by Cardenal, several members of the
Solentiname community went on to play a prominent role in the
overthrow of the Somoza dictatorship in the Sandinista revolution
of 1979, and the poet himself acted for a number of years as Minis-
ter of Culture in the first Sandinista government.

In all this time, however, the essence of Cardenal's vocation
remained that of the contemplative, and he alludes to this obliquely
in his poem "Reflections of a Minister," included in this volume,
where he describes seeing a cat by the roadside as he is about to
enter a reception at a foreign embassy. Rather than enter the
brightly lit embassy, Cardenal expresses the wish to remain outside
to observe the cat, "albeit in imitation of Marianne Moore /—that
cat of hers for example mouse in its mouth / tail dangling like a
shoe lace—." The reference is to the poem by Marianne Moore

titled "Silence," and although on the surface it seems that Cardenal simply wishes to capture the gentle humor of Moore's poem, if we go back to her full text we notice that she is quoting a piece of her own father's wisdom which includes the line "The deepest feeling always shows itself in silence." Many years ago Cardenal told me that the happiest time of his life had been the two years he spent in the Trappist monastery in Kentucky, and that the reason for this was the regime of silence that prevailed there, that gift of deep silence so longed for by contemplatives and mystics. A further indication of Cardenal's contemplative method of composition comes in the poem, "Destiny of an Insect," also included here, which describes a part of the poet's daily routine in which he would rest after lunch in a hammock under a porch at his home, with a pen and notebook by his side, ready to jot down the fruits of his meditation.

The second factor that may enhance our appreciation of Cardenal's poetry is an understanding of the artistic roots of his poetics. Cardenal is an American poet in the fullest sense. As defiantly American as the cosmopolitan Nicaraguan poet, Rubén Darío, who in 1905 threw down the gauntlet to the U.S. in his famous ode "To Roosevelt."[3] Legitimate heir though he is to Darío's poetics, Cardenal's discourse goes further and actually does appropriate the voice of the Bible and the verse of Walt Whitman.[4] In the late 1940s, Cardenal spent two years in graduate school at Columbia University, and exposure to the North American poetic tradition, from Whitman to Pound, to William Carlos Williams and to Marianne Moore, had a tremendous and lasting impact on his conception of how poetry should be written. We can recognize in Cardenal's work the simplicity of which Whitman wrote in his 1855 preface to *Leaves of Grass*: "The art of art, the glory of expression and the sunshine of the light of letters is simplicity. . . . nothing can make up for excess or for the lack of definiteness."

"Walt Whitman, a kosmos, of Manhattan the son" wrote in awe of the beauty of the cosmos and out of the belief in its interconnectedness: "I believe a leaf of grass is no less than the journey-work of the stars . . . And a mouse is miracle enough to stagger sextillions of infidels."[5] And reference to Whitman's mouse can be found in the notebooks Cardenal kept during his days at the Kentucky monastery.[6] However, in Cardenal's verse, the poetics have evolved with the incorporation of variations introduced by Pound, Williams, and Moore, among others. Note, for example, this observation by Grace Schulman in her introduction to the poems of Marianne Moore:[7]

> Marianne Moore's is emphatically an art of exact perception: to feel deeply is to see clearly, to peer beyond surfaces, and to explore permanent truths. The poet amasses facts, remarks, observations, details from guidebooks and manuals, in pursuit of answers to the mysteries of modern love, of nobility, of timeless values that she probes and probes again.

In Cardenal's extended poems, the form is very similar to this. There is a dynamic, cumulative effect in which fundamental beliefs and perceptions are constantly reinforced by a wealth of detail, both observed and culled from a staggeringly wide range of sources. The movement is that of a contemplative mindscape, a constant probing of the macro- and microcosmos for meaning and purpose; but in Cardenal there is less of the dark night of the soul and more of the visionary who perceives and celebrates the tenderness of love and human sexuality as an evolutionary driving force, as for example in the poem entitled "Vision in Grand Canary":

> *with thousands on the seafront avenue*
> *pressed up against each other*
> *you can hardly walk*
> *couples standing their skins as close together as possible*
> *delight of skin rubbing against skin*

And the beauty of the poetry lies in the verbal power that Cardenal is able to concentrate and sustain in his meditations, combined with a contemporary contemplative spirituality that is utterly engaged with the world. A revolutionary to the core, he introduces into his art a stripped-down, modern piety, a scientific piety that might have been the envy of St. John of the Cross. It is impossible to read these intensely human poems without being tremendously uplifted by the sheer affirmation of love and life.

John Lyons
São Carlos, Brazil, 2010

The Origin of Species

and Other Poems

The Origin of Species

That all life on earth
should come from a single cell:
            the great mystery
Everyone from a single ancestor
a universe still creating itself
         In the Galapagos
finches with different beaks
all had the same origin
but the islands divided them
             pincer-like beaks for insects
             sharp to perforate barks
             like tongs for harder seeds
                the thicker seeds
                thickened the beaks
Darwin thought that perhaps this happened
to all the birds in South America
and all the world's birds
         The whole of evolution like in the Galapagos

How does another species appear
Or biological diversity
            heron woman dragonfly
            millions of species
            all from the same origin
the beak of a bird
a little bigger
            through small variations
            the infinity of forms
one like a cow entered the sea
and became the whale
        Fish or mammal?
        Or mammal and fish
To Linnaeus a mammal
with a heart and lungs
and eyelashes that move
but with aquatic habits

Terrestrial mammals
that became sea ones
By adapting to the environment
          gradually
                    another species
fins of fish develop
into paws of invertebrates
                    why is one a parrot
                    and another a tiger
once there were no brains
now there are billions
there was no leaf
now everything is green
          From a single cell
                    trees animals you
                    all brothers
          we are all a modification of another
          the bird wing was dinosaur's paw
natural selection gradually
transforms the forms
like the beaks of the Galapagos
          The apes of Africa
          from which we come
The evolution of the eye the same
which even for Darwin was
"absurd in the highest possible degree"
          from a single photoelectric cell
          forty varieties of eye
but the complex organs
originate in small changes
          fins little by
          little become feet
          "to evolve" means
          to unroll a scroll
          and we cannot change direction

There are fossils of whales with whale
paws of terrestrial ancestors
and DNA tells us (in addition to fossils)

that the hippopotamus is close to them
just as we also know from DNA
that we are united to everything
to a mushroom for example
separated by mutation
and natural selection
>A billion and a half ago
>we separated from the mushroom
>through variation and inheritance
closer to the mushroom than to the carnation
>and we still have the vestiges of a tail

From such a simple origin
infinity of forms
walk crawl run skip swim fly
the mystery of this variety of life
all from the same ancestor
>Function creates the form
>and similar functions
>produce similar forms
thus the seeds changed
the beaks in the Galapagos
>"Stupid not to have thought of it before"
>said Huxley when he read
>*The Origin of Species*
small variation
in each generation
and from generation to generation
from gene to gene is evolution
and the beaks in the Galapagos change
>That such different species
>should have the same ancestor:
>why the horse and the bison
>with the same ancestor
>are so different?
>>Because one runs away
>>and the other attacks
>>>their forms separating
>>>in opposite direction

Microscopic algae
now immense trees
the gills become wings
and the arthropods took flight

Each tortoise was different
in each of the Galapagos islands
coming from the same tortoise

Graceful gazelle barely touching the ground
sloth with curved nails like a sickle
without tail and silky felt-like skin
frivolous butterfly in floral disguise
long-necked giraffe with unequal legs
Beneath the diversity of lives
all the same
dolphin fin and batwing
women breastfeed like seals
And biological diversity
occurs through gene exchange
—Darwin didn't know—
everything bound up in DNA
codified in the genes
which are as we now know
recipes for making a liver
a heart
and each cell knows its place
from 400 billion years ago
the first 200 just microbes
From there
the need for temporality
or time to pass
if not there'd be no evolution
nor future
DNA our Adam

The cosmos is natural selection
and some chance

                    (there'd be no evolution
                    if everything were chance
                    or if there were no chance)
And after all
the primordial origin
            is the subatomic particle
Inert matter became life
2 million years just bacteria
which appeared not to evolve
                    water covered the entire earth
                    and life was below the water
                    evolution was of microbes
                    and even now it is microscopic
(the bacteria within your gut
being altered by antibiotics)
            Single cell algae became forest
            and roots and wings developed
            The transition from fins to paws
            from life in water to life on earth

Parsimonious ant eater
with bird-like pointed snout
            hair-ball tail
peacock Sun King sunflower
                    the cautious cuautelo
                    pretending to be jaguar
ridiculous platypus
with duck-beaked snout
                    the elephant raises
                                its trunk like a trumpet
            zebra in prison stripes

We are so alike
variations on the same theme
our head is from the worm
or "we are all modified sharks"
the digestive process of an elephant
identical to that of a bacteria

the teeth with which I eat a lobster
are like those of the lobster
the invisible genes of an insect
        are those of our body
           which can only be explained
               by evolution
Everything observed on the *Beagle*
or in his microscope in England
and what he received in thousands of letters
He got to see few fossils but
each fossil was a missing link
and the whole Earth a huge museum
      He never wrote about religion

Insect bird reptile lily Einstein
since every transition is slow
every species appears without transition
but the whole of life is a single life
and in it there is a single Incarnation

      The rotten-leaf cicada
      Sleepy-eyed jaguar
      Squid with diadem of gems
lizard with dinosaur structure
aberrant wasp copulating with orchid
      the dromedary on its knees
           with its hump on its back
      the frog in its pond: ra ra ra ra
the heron with angel body
          and neck of snake
     ant carrying its gigantic leaf
         and the hummingbird's wingless flight
The same DNA in common
with all the animals
     and our hands and feet
     of amphibious fish and reptile
all emerged from the Big Bang
cosmos not finished yet

and every day is the Big Bang
    the creation-evolution continues
        traveling further and further away from nothing

My body you shaped from a worm
and then from a fish
cosmos with consciousness and transcendence
the cosmological miracle
of human presence in the cosmos

From the egg of a single cell
the animal with a billion cells
and the cell knows whether to make an eye
        or make a tongue
        a handful of cells go towards
        being a bird that flies

Darwin in the 600 pages
of *The Origin of Species*
speaks of the modifications
of species not the origin
the origin is a mystery
        that of the tiny fragile life
        in the immensity of dead worlds
                butterfly flower hummingbird
                girl dove whale
                the origin is love
                in different forms

        The hop hopping *zanatillo*
                        that hops along
        the spider with legs the color of air
        beating upon its web of threads of air
Iguana with its chlorophyll camouflage
wild flower with its Paris perfume
        string of silvery fish
                        like a piece of the sea
        aquatic flowers like ballet dancers

the elastic cat asleep
on the kitchen floor
the monkeys' vociferous hullabaloo
she known as Carmen in Granada
a small toad on a leaf
My God what a mystery
All from a single ancestor

Garden of shades of green
tiny shades at ground level
or at different heights
greens from which flowers emerge
of multiple colors and shapes:
how from a single plant
comes all this vegetation?
The new vision of Darwin:
that the infinite living beauty
had the same origin
and such a simple origin

Does a special species with
a special destiny exist?
(Question marks)
From hunter-gatherers
to global civilization
—The most recent in evolution—
Destiny that is God-evolution
a God who abandoned eternity
and has entered time
and is future?

The infinite future called God
a God who is the God of novelty
the infinite novelty of evolution
evolution against the status quo
that bankers desire so much

"God": imperfect conception
as the electron also is

without the electron being an illusion
The explanation of the Holocaust:
That to create he ceased to be God
Creation as *kenosis* (emptying
of God) impotent in the face of Pinochet
                    And a God not anthropomorphic
                    but one with whom I can talk

Much in common with mammals
and much in common with fish:
eyes the same and the same liver
        Greater still the union in the embryo:
        quadruped and fish in the same embryo
        although us without gills after

Life emerged on land
and began to walk
slippery fish
leaning on fins
        like crutches
                        from the aquatic limit
        to the limitless air
when a well dries
        it survives
walking to another well
                and the fins became paws

The great mystery of life
all sharing the same origin
and that such different bodies
should come from a single cell
all species relatives
        from orchids to earthworms
        bacteria gradually dinosaurs
        then the dinosaur became bird
        also our mollusk ancestor
                        There is only one animal
In a non-local quantum universe
where we are interconnected

despite the immense distances
            Will annihilation be
            the end of the universe?

Evolution unites us all
the living and the dead
Darwin discovered it
            (that we come from a single cell)
that is we are interlinked
            if one rises from the dead
            we all rise from the dead

Manaus Resurrected

I thought it did not exist
swallowed up by the forest
now merely a ghost city
                    Manaus
with its opera house for Caruso
and the clothes sent to be washed in London
Carrara marble from Italy
Custom house brought from Liverpool
with numbered stones
        the brewery a Bavarian castle
                the most sumptuous city in America
                second or third to have electric light
closer ties to London than to Rio de Janeiro
immense harbor of floating steel
brought floating from London
        with horse races and regattas
        luminous fountains and metallic bridges
        Belgian cycle tracks and German bowling alleys
                whores from the Moulin Rouge
the shirts come back pressed from London
        the tigers close to casinos and clubs
vulgar criminals in dress coats in the brothels
        alongside the quagmires the Versaillesque
                the Paris of the forest
        with its tiled boulevards
and the ephemeral splendor of the Florentine Theater
blood and sweat of the rubber tappers
the theater boxes with little banisters of gilded iron
and the electric light of the chandeliers
reflected in the Venetian mirrors
the forest painted onto the huge drop-curtain
and real around Manaus
fountain of pink angels and rococo roses
                golden cupolas
                        little squares with booths

belle époque style
the London Stock Market ended it all

Later the forest crept back in
                    instead of gala costumes
                                    lizards in the Amazon Theater
the dome with nymphs and goddesses
no longer echoing to Sarah Bernhardt
                    without electric light but plenty of mosquitoes
boas in the mini-Versailles
trousseaux no longer brought in from Paris
            nor boats with Italian operettas
the boats now only for those who were leaving
            making obscene gestures at Manaus
the rubber boom lasted so few years
Manaus reverted once more to the long-drawn lethargy
of the Amazonian cities
            the locomotive immobilized between the lianas
                    and like the yellow fever that kills the monkeys
                    was the fall in the price of rubber for Manaus

But now it has become a Free Zone
for all commerce in Amazonia
                    an industrial Eden we could say
        luxurious forest of domestic appliances
                        and glass skyscrapers
and to my surprise I saw a lively metropolis
        schoolgirls getting off buses
and scattered like pigeons in the square
with its wave-shaped mosaic paving
in front of the marble façade of the Amazon Theater
        Manaus's noisy traffic
                    hotels
                                planes arriving
                the din of car horns
buildings with incomprehensible graffiti
by mysterious young people we never see
that we see everywhere today

I catch the smell of fish
from Manaus's market
the market a lacework of iron
like the Eiffel Tower
and built also by Eiffel
the fish on the marble slabs
pirarucú   tucunaré   tambaquí
and a thousand more
pirarucú the size of a man
salted and rolled up like a carpet
tambaquí fat like a pig and tasting of pork
tucunaré that Thiago took us to eat
in a working-class restaurant
crisply fried in scalding pork fat

invited on this first occasion by Thiago de Mello
a native of Amazonia
to his house downriver
24 hours by boat from Manaus
the governor lent us his boat
and I traveled in the governor's cabin
the waters of the Rio Negro
like dark glasses
the wake the color of very strong tea
way in the distance the mid-river banks
greeny-blue the closest one
the furthest one bluey-green
blurred because of the haze and the distance
but they're not the banks of the river but
of islands beyond which
there are other islands and other branches of the river
also small floating islands downriver
bigger than the boat
riverbanks disappeared and appeared in another stretch
a small two-story boat abandoned
beached on a bank where the water carried it
houses on rafts or on tall stakes on the river
surrounded by palm trees and papayas

                    colorful clothes drying
                              next to the latrine
          in old broken boats full of earth
          rows of vegetables or flowers
the small launches with palm roofs like huts
          vegetation of every shade of green
          soft almost yellow green of the grasses
          dark almost black green of the trees
and just for a moment
in a bend
                    between the two shores
                    a glimpse
                              of the entire Amazon
                                        an ocean!
Pink dolphins are trailing us

Barreirinha
          Where Thiago has his house
Next to an imposing river
                    the Andirá:
          a mere tributary of the Amazon
and there close to Thiago's place
          in the little boat they lent us to fish
          we caught only piranhas
                    multicolored
          with gleaming scales
                              that we ate roasted
in an Indian village
                    the young men in a terrible wager
                                        drunk with pain
                    to see who could bear the most ants
and back to Manaus again
the Meeting of Amazonian Poets
me invited as an honorary Amazonian poet
          when we read poems in a huge park
                    to crowds of people
and also in the forest
having as backdrop a landscape where the Amazon

and the Rio Negro meet
and once more in Manaus
the re-inauguration of the Amazon Theater
        hugely expensive restoration of a dream
        everything just as it was before
and my poetry reading
                        which I could hardly believe
        in that dream Theater
and now Manaus is no longer a ghost city
where I am even a member of the Amazonian Academy
The London Stock Exchange put an end to it all
but your Manaus Thiago has risen from the dead

Elegy for Cristina Downing

Cristina my mother's cousin
was fifteen then
    tiny waist
    skinny shins I remember
    and I was seven years old
              it was the era
              of Doña Carmela Noguera
              Joaquín Pasos wrote
                    (Doña Carmela she
                    of the school soirées
                    where as a schoolgirl
                    Cristina shone)
and it was the era of Greta Garbo
Lindbergh Babe Ruth Chaplin
              girlfriend to the vanguardista poets
    she didn't stay a fifteen year old
    nor I a child
          her last years
          between four walls
          she remembered nothing
          not even who she was

Babe Ruth with his home runs
was when I was a child
    maybe you don't know who he is
he died way back
Dickinson said:
If I shouldn't be alive
Give the one in Red Cravat,
A Memorial crumb
    Merton died
the stars will die without heat
cold like their surroundings
and Eliot: "they all go into the dark"
    The black holes also disappear
In my poetry workshop

for children with cancer
a child wrote
about doomed children
waiting their turn
                Everyone in the cosmos
                waiting their turn

Orphans in a mechanistic world
at the mercy of accidents and chance
                the Ford I climb into
                could be the death of me
What is life
                made of particles
                elemental particles
                that are not alive?
"that's the way the world is"
we all say
quantum mechanics has proved
that it's not how it is
or computers would not work
        Just as we grow old
        we should ungrow old
                there's no symmetry
        this asymmetry of time
                where did it come from?
where did we come from
children of time
surrounded by perishable beauty
longing for everlasting beauty?

If there is a God we're immortal
        and if not we're not
        that's all there is
                there's no other alternative
                to being eternal
                or eternally not being
eternity or nothing that's it
only the short time we were alive

merely those days gone by
and there'll never ever be anything else
nothing else for ever and ever
being nothing for all eternity

        One day consciousness
        turned upon itself
        consciousness of itself
        and unfortunately
        of its death
Only animal that knows it's going to die
    There had to be consciousness
    that could grasp the universe
    And grasping the universe
    knew that we died
The appearance of consciousness
was another biological existence
    Not merely knowing but knowing oneself
    not just knowing but knowing one knows
The certainty of death
as fruit of that advance
Animals know
but not themselves
to know oneself
was to know we die
    Consciousness a danger to the species
    To be able to survive the certainty of death
    and despite it not to have become extinct

Hunter-gatherer
in the black forest
    without doctors
the slightest malaise
induced fear
        and among lions
        defenseless and naked
        walking food
    cut the berries

looking all around
afraid of death
  gazing at the beautiful stars
  without understanding them
  what could they be?
Hunter-gatherers
conscious of being conscious
  conscious of death
    the wounded deer died
      and the killer knew
    that he would die too

Up above in the branches
there was no death
    The monkey inhabits the present
      intensely
    with no past
        and no future
Nor does death exist for children
who would be children forever!
    When I was four
    I killed a parakeet with a coconut
    and I screamed at what I'd done
      (that's how I discovered death)

    In the black forest
    where anything can happen
    death is the only
    certainty we have
Ever since humanity has existed there have been
religions
    superstitions if you like?
    Or maybe
      it was faith
This way we did not become extinct
knowing that we died

There is a God or the universe is absurd
And if there is not we die forever

This would be the meaning of transcendence
an adaptation of evolution in the mind
our species' defense mechanism
in the face of the paralyzing effect of consciousness
of death
                    Thus we survive
Religions or superstitions
          it was always faith
in immortality

The day will come
when there will be no astronomy
and the sky will be empty
the galaxies separate
and become isolated
no other galaxy in sight
and in each lonely galaxy
the stars dying out
and when the last dies
all will be deep darkness
          (this isn't science fiction)
If that's the way it is Cristina Downing
there's no salvation in this cosmos
                              Save
                    for a biological miracle
                    —the Incarnation—
                    A biological evolution
                    that culminates in God

We are a single Body
that of one who rose again
from among the dead
                    Humanity is one
                    organically one
                    if one rises again
                    we all rise again
"If He has not risen we're fucked"
                         1 Corinthians 15:17

Evolution has a direction
which is the union of the universe:
the Love of a humanity without loneliness
incompatible with total death
All determined which is why it is said:
"So that the Scriptures may be fulfilled"
It wasn't prophesied because it would happen
rather it happens because it was prophesied
                    All rise again
                        those that are one
            in a past future present
Cristina Downing
                    P r e s e n t !
Or maybe it will be like being born again:
a new life in a new universe

            The Scriptures say
            he had to die
            to rise again

Theory of Language

We were going to go in a group
and the telephone in my hotel room:
"We're ready to leave"
This miracle of speech!

5 words
Perfect expression
said so quickly and with such ease
Who invented language?
How did we start to speak?
Linguists have no answer.
First just words alone
with no connection between them.
Some stick together:
two together a new meaning.
Three signify more.
Woman red fruit
the order also signifying
and so a grammar appeared
still lacking any elegance.

Why language so complex?
Simpler would be better? With
individual words and little vocabulary without
syntax
like someone who speaks a language badly
'Me avocado want'
or *broken English*
Separate, isolated words
without *to* and without *and*
without *after*, without *because*.
But, no, complexity of language
was chosen
syntactic structure
rules and grammatical categories
to avoid ambiguity.
Words express us.

Syntax is the relationship between them:
it accelerates communication.
What's bad is ambiguity.

We gave a name to everything.
Individual words came first.
Names for the real and the imaginary.
Naming made us human.
Animals don't name.
Nor do they know their names.
They circulate in a confused reality
without ideas and without names.

There was no syntax
until there were many names.
To say *he* or *she*
saves many words.
The mind evolved
to capture complexity.
Morphology and syntax, what made us human.
And this is how I can write this.
The genes for speaking better are inherited
and that was the evolution of language:
More and more complex syntax
to speak better.
Handing language down from
generation to generation.
In the midst of animals that do not talk.
Structure of the brain
and structure of language
the 2 big mysteries.
(language is already there in the embryo).
Okay. But although there is a computer
in the tiny head of birds
our brain, larger than it should be,
is the biggest computer in the world.

This magic of language.
When we hear the sound from a mouth

which is only a fluctuating buzz
and a harmonious air turbulence
we immediately distinguish the meaning
and we hear the separate words
Do you want a McDonald's too?
although no silence separates them
(if it's a language that we don't understand
we don't perceive the separation of words).
And the immense power of speech
even in a rudimentary form
absent in the other species.
Song came first.
Song is pleasing even without understanding the words.
Communication generates imitation
and song was imitated
and from this, language.
Song came first
because singing is easier.
Could it have been maternal lullaby?
                    Love song.
In any case
love created language.
Really?

It appears the first language was song.
Like the song of birds or whales?
Birds don't sing
                    says Robbins Burlin
nor whales. They lack
the metronomic beat of human music.
It's not music if it doesn't have equal beats
synchronized with the dance
which it frequently accompanies.
We accompany music with the foot and
not the sound of mammals or prose, he says.
In music we clap in time
anticipating the moment when the others clap.
And likewise dance or military march.

Not even circus horses
learn to keep step
when running or trotting he says.
In short: birds don't sing.
Interesting Jespersen's comment:
  Love inspired songs
  and this is the origin of language.

Natural selection selected
the best speaker and the best listener
to be chiefs or to get a partner
and so through the millennia
language evolved.
Language that is not in our genes
but which we have to learn.
      Children
little linguists.
Language created over millions of years
by natural selection.
Small changes introduced
proceed from one generation to the next
until it is another language
and also slang or jargon.
Language also by selection.
  A strange primate that speaks!

We are not an evolving chimpanzee
but something similar
evolving.
And so
we argue, we joke, we beg, we woo
and we lie.

This implausibility that is speech
  Words in phrases
    and phrases within phrases
    subject verb predicate
eons of evolution of language

and now we are born with grammar.
Our last evolution, that
of the larynx
which made us human.
We have a "language organ"
it seems.
      Chatting over tea and cakes
      nothing to do with monkeys.
Smiles, sighs, kisses:
words without syntax.
There are species with sounds
          growls howls
             a gentle warble among the leaves
     the song of the frogs beneath the moon
     and its echo
         non-symbolic communication of the non humans
but which they cannot do using syntax
         so easy for children!

In 1979 the Nicaraguan
deaf-mutes
brought together by the Revolution
not knowing sign-language
—there was no one to teach them—
created their own language
(a moustache was Daniel Ortega)
with complicated grammar and with
declensions as in Latin and with
hyperbaton,
very versatile prepositions and verbs
as with the Navajos.
A new language appeared
the newest language in the world
that the deaf-mute children invented.
A linguist said: "A unique case
in history. We have witnessed the birth
of a language." And one linguist:
"A linguist's dream."

A remarkable natural experiment
                                        said Chomsky
confirmation of his theory
of biological grammar
and that we are born with syntax.
                    The Nicaraguan Sign Language
                    Linguists from all over the world
                    have studied this language.
Yes, we are born knowing how to speak.
Humanity means having language.
There has never been a tribe without speech
and it differentiates our species
to be forever talking.
Miracle of the name made thing.
A true mystery:
                    a sound and a thing.
Names of things through
the concepts of things.
                    Linguistic evolution:
Natural selection favors
those who speak more clearly
or understand better.
These reproduce more.
Language genes
(complex genes)
to speak and to understand.
                            Did language create the mind
                            or the opposite?
To speak you need to think
        and vice versa
in other words
                            to speak is to think
                            to think is to speak
if we did not speak we would not think.
Only our ancestors managed it.
Others are aerodynamic
so as to fly or to swim.
Speech is also the lie, the slander

and war
(to speak and to write).

Impossible to communicate with other species
but might we not through radio-telescope
   across space
with planets of other stars?

"We are ready to leave"
    marvelous invention
  if not
  there'd be no communication among ourselves
nor with God.

Manaus Revisited

Jungle of skyscrapers
white all white
I calculated something like one hundred
but according to Thiago there are more than one hundred
when the sun strikes them head on
they glisten like snow
      vertical city
huge avenues with rivers of cars
      their red and white lights
      coming and going
the sun setting over the Rio Negro
which after Manaus becomes the Amazon
      between the skyscrapers
         green areas
         of Amazon jungle
    tall tall trees
    infinite shapes of palm tree
    the entire space full of leaves
    strategies to capture the light
from my hotel balcony on the 20th floor
the city stretching out to the horizon
at the end the blue strip of the Rio Negro
and by night it will shine like the firmament
        what was once a ghost city

Descendants of hunter-gatherers
who came to be what we are today
never imagining they would build cars
    skyscrapers computers
technology is also biological
    like carapace or shell
our descendants could be made of silicon
      or alloy

but would retain what is human
as we do the brain of the alligator

I am in Manaus again
for a meeting of Amazon writers
(they consider me Amazon too)
        I've eaten pirarucú once again
and once again I observe though way in the distance
the golden cupola of the Amazon Theater

Reflections on the River Grijalva

          Immense   immense
like Colorado's Grand Canyon I think
but between two forests
two very deep
          or tall
                        forests
    below the green river snak-
    ing like the ser-
          pent of quetzal feathers
famous canyon which the poet Pellicer never
liked
I don't like it he said
    But why not?
Because it's not in Tabasco he said
and because the river actually winds through Tabasco
                        his Tabasco
after Chiapas
but the canyon's in Chiapas and not in Tabasco
    almost perpendicular the forest
    on both sides of the river
you gaze down at the small launch from the observation deck
          as from a plane
and from the launch
          the observation deck amid the clouds
          as though it's about to topple down on you
    the view from on high with such vegetation so
    different from that below with the same vegetation
this is where an entire tribe
before the astonished Conquistadors' very eyes
          so the legend says
hurled themselves into the abyss
    and now it's an observation deck
the best panorama in the world
                  says the tourist guide

at the entrance to the canyon there are remains
of a Chiapan ceremonial center

Here is the habitat of the quetzal and the Zapatistas
of the symbolic jaguar
      and the heron with its questioning neck
          also of the toucan
      the curassow with its caricatured bird face
specimens of monkey and alligator can be observed
the spider monkey that is amused by the strange
          habits of humanity
nervous white-tailed deer that approach you
      and other neotropical species
      in the ecotourist park
          with observation decks and picnic spots
      souvenirs and postcards in the snack bar
the geological formation is
at least 12 million years old
      touch the rock
          you can feel the years
and the hard and gentle texture of the Ceiba
I breathe in the wind from the 4 cardinal points
      that converge on this place
I watch the pelicans
        as though on air command maneuvers
      and there's the mysterious rain tree
      that wets you as you pass under it even if it's not raining
below the sheer cliffs
flow the rapids and torrents
into which the Chiapas Indians threw themselves

                Well

we traveled along that river
      a tourist trip
between the two vertical forests
of super abundant tropical vegetation
low deciduous forest and evergreen forest
the sedimentary strata with caves and waterfalls

                the sky reflected motionless
                in the fleeting water
that flows towards Tabasco and the Gulf of Mexico
liquid glass or transparent plastic
                but it splashes
                                on the seats at the front
a snap of the sky and a snap of the tall vertical
                                                forests
                but suddenly
at a bend
of the river
                        a pool of paralyzed water
                                fetid carpet
        of detergents coca-cola ketchup shampoos Kellogg Tabasco
        chile bottles plastic bags bags bags Colgate toothpaste
        Gillette cream tires empty packaging Eau de Cologne open
        cans Listerine box of Kleenex piece of shoe dead cat rags
        Kotex cardboard plates cans of paint toys broken vase . . .

all floating
                        in the gentle sway of the water
                maybe a kilometer of garbage
the speed boat slowly navigating among the buzzards
until finally it emerges from
                that Avernus of fetid products
of every kind of label
                                the corpse of a Supermarket
here they retain the garbage
before the hydroelectric dam
                        and once again the clear water
                        mimicking the sky and the forest
                                until the huge hydroelectric plant which
                                provides power to Mexico and Central America
                and the end of this excursion

        But
                        back home
                                        I think

Could the universe not care less
about the ecological anxieties
of just a few mad fools?
Or does the universe cry out through us?
Might there not be some meaning to it all
or is it an entirely meaningless world?
If we emerged from irrational matter
as the atheist materialists say
and we return to irrational matter
children of an irrational nature
and its irrational natural selection
does it matter what we do or don't do?

           let us buy and buy in the Supermarkets
           because tomorrow dear heart we die
because the question
    as to whether there's a purpose or not
              in the universe
      even though we don't know we do it
      affects our daily life
the clear or dirty waters of the Grijalva
            what does it matter
      if tomorrow we will die
and if all that awaits us is the emptiness
         at the end of the process
there are thinkers who think
that to think of a purpose
is archaic
      and all cosmic teleology
      a psychological projection
      in a meaningless universe
      its evolution directionless
    the evolution of an eye not knowing what it will see!
    and that the mind is conscious merely by accident

If the end of everything is total extinction
            it's all unnecessary
      if there is no Eternity
           it's fucking pointless

apparently
in an indifferent universe
or in the merely accidental one
"the scientific model of the universe"
                                        is without us
a concept of the universe without humans
            and a cosmos that is not our home
                because if what's "real" is what's contained in classical physics
                    we are exiled in the cosmos
reality reduced to matter without life
of a physics now superseded
                            without the unnecessary hypothesis
                            of God
            with the unconscious con-
viction that we are not cosmos
and unconscious of being interdependent
that everything is interrelated with everything
                all of us in a single All
is what makes us indifferent
to the environment
                the flora and fauna lost forever

But it's not like that rather
since everything is related to everything
human destiny does not
differ from that of the entire universe
                    every entity is relationship
            relationship is the true substance of being
                        and even the Trinity is relationship
atoms aren't the same observed
as not observed
which is why we are not unnecessary in the cosmos
But are we observers important
with our lavish waste in this tiny corner?
Who cares what's thrown into the Grijalva?
        Or is there someone further removed from the cosmos
                                who weeps

                        beyond space
                        and before time
              at what we are now destroying?
What we do to the world affects God
And whoever offends another offends God

Are we going to die? So what
others will come afterwards
        our relief
                            what joy!
And but for death they'd never come
the girl who today takes her photos
wouldn't be there but for the dead
                the universe is not cruel
                nor nature hostile
                                and yes it is severe
        but in order to evolve
evolution is born from conflict
neither is reality absurd
in fact we have to see the relationship
        between our ecological vision
        and our cosmovision
Do religions not say that
we are not of this earth
                                or kind of exiles
        or that we have to free ourselves from matter?
Certainly beauty is transient
but the resurrection is not solely
for immortal souls alone
without matter and without history
we love time
in which mangoes and girls mature
        but not the time which causes all things to pass
                —and which poets so much lament—
that all things pass to the past
        but even though they pass
they are preserved in the past
and from there they will return again

                    provided there is resurrection
because if not
                as Saint Paul said
we're fucked

                But
                if the universe
                had a beginning
                it is not eternal
                                and that
                                's very good
because something new will be born
                even though this
                new thing
                is a mystery

Iquitos Zoo

After observing the Amazonian animals
    the big lounging leopard
        yellow with black quadrilaterals
miniscule monkeys play-acting
        at fights in the branches
the parrots wrapped in flags
the sloth with its terrifying claws
            but weak
the outlandish toucan with its sharp beak
    like the false-bird-of-paradise
                (Heliconias)
the boa thick as a firehose
    uncoiling itself
        decorated with Incan borders
the elongated alligator
and its rugged topography with high peaks
the rapturous tortoises each one on its stone
the elastic otter stretched to its limit
—the nine-year-old Indian guide
picked up from the ground a huge
            red petal
    that had fallen from a tree
        and said to me:
"Touch it, it's soft as a leopard's skin"
and certainly it was soft as the silky skin with
    black quadrilaterals
           that we didn't touch.

The White Goddess

The reason I was in that
out-of-the-way little village in Majorca
one Mediterranean midday was
a book bought not long before
in the Columbia University bookshop
in New York: *The White Goddess* by Robert Graves
which is about nothing less than
                        the discovery of a goddess.

He proves with devastating erudition
that in pagan and still matriarchal Europe
there was only one great goddess whom
all the peoples worshipped. A mother
goddess with a son also god. Goddess
of virginity and procreation, fertility
and death, love and terror, of heaven
and hell. With the later establishment of the Asian
patriarchy, the god her first son, and many other
subsequent gods, took the place of the goddess.
But belief in her never entirely disappeared.
It endured in the countless myths, legends and
superstitions of all the peoples, which persist
to this day. Venus, Diana, the Graces,
the Muses, nymphs, sirens, Circe, are
fragments of the Great Goddess myth. The
tales of sorcery and witches everywhere,
women who appear in the night to destroy men,
the spider woman, the woman who sucks men's
blood and whose embrace is death . . . The Goddess
always has the same physical appearance according to Graves:
white, beautiful and slim, pale, pointed
nose, long and beautiful hair, lips
bright red and light blue eyes. Botticelli painted her
exactly in the *Birth of Venus,* says Graves.
Shakespeare knew and feared her, and she is Keats's

Belle Dame Sans Merci. Death
                       which confers poetic immortality.

She is the white mare of the night: *nightmare*
and she is serpent and siren and witch. Above
all the Goddess myth is one with the moon
(the moon that is woman with normal menstrual cycle
of twenty-eight days). And a remnant of this cult
is what we currently know as poetry
                       —but also dance, music and magic—.
Poetry that sends a shiver with an owl whistle,
moon racing between the clouds, trees swaying, a few
dogs barking in the distance:
                       it's due to the Goddess's presence.
In the beginning the poet led the religious dances.
His verses were danced around an altar
and each verse was a new round of dance,
whence *versus* in Latin which means round,
and *ballad* is a danced poem (from *baillare,* to dance).
The dances were seasonal, from which the single universal
theme of poetry was born: life and death and resurrection
of the Spirit of the Year, son and lover of the Goddess.

                    That's why
poetry is always tied to the moon
and to woman. Since Homer there has never been, says Graves,
a true poet who has not sung to that divine and
terrifying woman. The one who in primitive times was
the sole great Goddess. Poets even now
continue to invoke her with the name of Muse
and this is the language of true poetry.
Although "myth" today is tantamount to absurd or anti-historical.
The poet is measured according to the accuracy with which he describes
the White Goddess and her island.

                    The Triple Muse.
And Triple Goddess: of Heaven, Earth and Hell.

The moon in its three phases: new, full and waning
which as new moon or spring was a girl,
as full moon or summer was a woman
and as waning moon the winter a witch.
The Triple Goddess was also the three Graces
and the nine Muses that were initially three.
                              And she was the sole Goddess:
                    Rhea the Virgin Goddess mother of Zeus
                       who later transformed into the Virgin Mary
                          became the Queen of Heaven again.
Graves preferred Catholicism to Protestantism
because of Mary, beloved by the troubadours and who
for so many centuries has inspired so much art.

The language of myths and symbols was simple
says Graves, and in time it became confused.
Apollo imposed reason above poetry, and still it
continues to be imposed in schools and universities:
instead of the magical language of poetry
the rational and classical in honor of Apollo.
And poetry declined. But the true poet
is he who sings to the Muse (not to the King or to the people).
Woman should not be parted from the poets.
The Apollonians seek to do this, and they fall
into sentimental homosexuality. Homosexual
Platonism drives poets out of the city.
True poetry is invocation of the White Goddess
or Muse.

                    Woman is Muse or she is nothing. Woman
                    is always Muse, even if she writes poetry.

(Or as Coronel later remarked to me, when
we were crossing the lake in a launch one night:
"What we already knew: Just as Mary is intermediary
of all the supernatural graces, woman

is intermediary of all the natural graces." In the launch one night
under a full moon which turned the lake moon-color).

So it was a very special book about woman, by
a man certainly very much in love with his wife.
About whom not long before *Time* had said: "He is one
of the most intelligent and erudite men
in the world." And it was the book I'd been reading
on the sun-lounger on deck, watching the wake
from the stern
                —Poseidon's curly hair—
of the French boat heading for Le Havre. From
New York to Le Havre. My first trip to Europe.
And this was the reason why I was now
on this blue Mediterranean midday in
the out-of-the-way village of Deyá, Majorca
where Robert Graves lived, and the reason why
book in hand I knocked on his door.

I'd come by bus from Palma de Majorca
along a road lined with old twisted
olive trees and flowering almonds. I stopped
first at Valldemossa's Carthusian monastery, Chopin's
and Rubén's monastery, with Chopin's Playel piano
and the window through which Rubén in Carthusian habit
would enter to wander through the solitary cloisters.
From the same balcony as Rubén
I observed the sheer mountains of pine and olive trees
and a field with peasant women picking olives.
And I later observed
the beautiful Majorcan peasant women dancing
with a passion I'd never seen in any other dance, which
made me think just how primitive Spain
still was. The deeply religious or maybe mystical
fervor of the boys and girls
pounding and pounding the earth, just as
twenty-five centuries earlier the boys and girls
in these same places and wearing similar

costumes had pounded and pounded and pounded
to produce the fertility of the land or
      to make it rain,
            at the feet of a Goddess.

Then I saw Miramar, one of the most beautiful sea-
scapes in the world. A radiant blue sea
seen from the coast which descends perpendicularly
almost, covered in pure pines which shoot up
directly from the beachless sea shore.
            The winedark sea . . .
When I saw the Mediterranean for the first time
it was in Valencia, and Fr. Beltrán, a Valencian:
"This is the sea of Venus, Homer, Ulysses and the sirens"
while we were heading towards the lighthouse . . . And it was totally smooth
smooth without a wave but for a tiny ripple almost
imperceptible on the shore. Like our lake
on its best days (the May calms)
            although without a heron.

Once again I remembered Homer, Ulysses, Venus, sirens
from the sheer vantage point of Miramar beside a
half-ruined red tower, and the sea breeze brought back to me
lines Rubén wrote on this island which he loved and where
they worship him as though they were Nicaraguans or
he was from Majorca:
         "I know that with vine shoots and roses crowned
         the Muses here once danced before the sea"

And then some 20 minutes from Miramar, now
close to midday, the bus dropped me at the entrance
to Deyá, where I was going to visit Robert Graves.
I asked at the minuscule telegraph office
at the town entrance, and the telegraphist in more
Mallorquin than Spanish: "At the end of the village after
a curve there are some bungalows, the last but one
belongs to the secretary, the next one, to Mr. Graves."
I walked through the little village with small houses on either

side of a road that twisted as it climbed or
scattered in the valley below, and beyond the final curve
I passed the house that must have been the secretary's and
I stopped at the next one with its small garden
that must have been Graves's. Ahead a ravine and in the distance
a patch of sea. At this moment
I hesitated to enter, because it was now almost
midday, and if they ate early it would be lunch
time. In any case, I decided to knock, as
I was at the door, and ask whoever opened it
if it was not an inopportune time, or at what time
the writer could receive me. A tall, well-built
man opened the door, with unkempt graying hair
and in a country suit like one of those
gamekeepers in English novels. I
recognized him: "You are Robert Graves I presume . . . "
"Yes, come in and eat with us." It was a
typical well-ventilated country house, untidy, where
you can see there are children and you feel at home.
At the table the wife and four children were finishing
their meal, and she not taking no for an answer served me
a plate of chicken soup with vegetables while
I explained to Graves that I was from Nicaragua and had come
about his book *The White Goddess,* which I was carrying in my hand.
He fetched the globe in the living room and spun it
round until placing his finger on Nicaragua and
he called the children so they could see where
I was from: "Here we are . . .
and here is Nicaragua." And the children bent over to see
the tiny Mediterranean spot where they were,
and the other equally tiny spot, amazed
that it was so far away. "Wow!"

While I ate my soup
I gave him a review to read which I'd written
about his book recently published in Madrid. "I'll show you
other chapters I've added. I discovered that the cult
of the Goddess was taken by Spain to England and Ireland and

that Majorca was a very important site
for this cult." After some cognacs and while
his wife was clearing the table he took me to his office.
"In this study I wrote *The White Goddess.*
These are the drafts." I was surprised how small
his book collection was, almost like mine, a student.
How could he write about all the myths and legends
of the world? "Here I keep only what's most important. The
rest my secretary fetches for me or I request it in London. For
example I have a Jewish friend in the largest
Jewish library in the world."

                                    Back in the living room
I told him stories of the White Goddess in Nicaragua.
The Cegua (*cíhuatl* in Nahuatl, which means woman)
a very beautiful woman who seduced men in the night
to destroy them, and suddenly she becomes hideous:
the skin a maize husk and the teeth grains of maize.
Carmen Aseada on her island in Lake Nicaragua,
the terror of sailors, who unleashed storms and sudden calms
to entice men to her island and never let them leave.
Like Circe in the Mediterranean (whose name is *circle*
according to Graves, because of the magic circle that surrounded her) each
morning she drew a circle with her white finger in the sand
and her chickens, all white, could not leave
that circle. Very white and very beautiful and so clean
that her urinating and drinking vessel was the same.
He tells me: "Quite certainly on this island there was an oracle
and probably a temple dedicated to the Goddess
where men were sacrificed. That's what it was like
with the Mediterranean sirens."

                                    He interrupted our chat
to give the children a lesson in Latin and set them
their Greek homework. "They go to school in the morning
but Latin and Greek I teach them.
With their mother they speak English and Spanish, but
together only Mallorquin." After the class
he and his wife, also intelligent and well-educated,
told me about the literary London

of their day: Eliot, Auden, poor Spender
homosexual ("But surely everyone knows!" And the wife
confirmed it). He was surprised that I, devoted to the Goddess,
should like the poetry of the homosexual Whitman. I should
have told him that he was gay but a Dionysian
and not Apollonian. And returning to the Goddess:
"What are the women like in your country? Because in England
they are culturally active. They hang around with writers
and artists. Attend their meetings. In Majorca
since they cannot go out alone they don't participate. Women
never enter the cafés where the *tertulias* take place.
I tell you something" he says standing up: "When
women are present in culture culture flourishes. When
not, there is decadence." I told him that in Nicaragua
women used to be like in Majorca, but now
we'd managed to get some of them to join us
(in my mind Mimí Hammer and others). He signed
the book I had brought

> *With great friendship* (in Spanish).

There was a sort of toy mandolin of the children's
and he started to play it. I asked him if you could be a poet
without a musical ear. "Yes you can, although the troubadours
generally accompanied themselves with an instrument."
When it was time for me to leave, he, with his wife and
children who were also going to the village, accompanied me.
On the way I asked him: "Are these laurels?"
He turned around to look at them astonished and then it hit him: "Ah
yes, you don't have these in America!" And he continued to point out
classic plants to me on the way. "This is acanthus. These are broad beans
the plant of immortality consecrated to the Goddess. They
placed them on the dead. The Romans never eat them for this reason.
The flowers at the front of the house are periwinkles
which was the flower of Death."

Later I often recalled my chat with Graves
and his book, traveling through other parts of Europe where
there are still remnants and signs of the White Goddess. A small
oratory with a dilapidated fountain dedicated to the nymphs

in the center of Rome. A small round temple of vestals
consecrated to Diana in Tivoli. The ruins of an Etruscan
theatre in Fiesole, close to Florence, where boys
and girls on a picnic adorned themselves with leaves
for a game—classic plants of which Graves would know
all the symbols—and they began to dance boy
with girl in the old theatre in jest, but
moved by who knows what ancestral impulse, and to play
at bullfighting, and I thought of the virgin
priestesses who fought white bulls naked at night
in solitary amphitheaters by the light of the moon
as told in *Tutankhamen in Crete*. And later Capri
full of vineyards and olive groves, and with its almond trees
in flower sweetening the air. Capri that was the island of
the sirens, who according to what Homer tells sang
in a meadow white from the bones of men:
Come closer Ulysses . . . ! Halt your boat so you may hear our song!

The White Goddess I also met, and many times,
in Paris. The first with the discovery of a
real siren. Not just sirens in slacks and tight-fitting
multi-colored sweaters, coming
and going at all hours in merry groups along
the Boulevard Saint Germain—which are real too—
but the photograph of a real siren, fished
in India and with a scientific name: *Aliquorae*
indicus. We were returning from the Seine to our small hotel Carlos
Martínez and I, and we saw in a shop window what
we thought must be some African fetish,
a kind of really frightening witch with claws,
but it was a photo of a fish from India
with the head of a woman and arms ending in claws
and with breasts to suckle its infants. It measured
two and a bit meters and weighed 200 pounds. This dissected
specimen was in the Paris Natural History Museum.
And nobody in Paris had given it the slightest importance,
as far as we knew, nor had there been publicity of the fact
of having a dissected siren in the museum. We told,

I remember, Monique Fong, a beautiful half-Chinese 19-year-old
friend, in the Café des États-Unis, and she was astonished
and said she'd tell André Breton in the *tertulia*
over which he pontificated and which she attended. Another time
it was in the Louvre where Carlos and I also discovered
extremely rare white abstract sculptures with curves
in the form of violin or like primitive axes of
well polished stone, Brancusi *avant* Brancusi
although the museum label merely said that
they were found on Mediterranean islands and were
idols: "violin-shaped" and "disk-shaped idols."
From the violin curves we convinced ourselves
that they were female forms and therefore
of the White Goddess—the Louvre that merely called
them violin- and disk-shaped idols certainly wasn't
aware of this—and so from then onwards with every visit
to the museum it was obligatory to walk past glancing at them.
It so happened by chance that in those days *Time* magazine
ran the photos of some figures recently
found on the island of Sardinia exactly the same
as ours in the Louvre, and it said they were of a goddess
that had been worshipped throughout the Mediterranean.
Reaching the village my chat with Robert Graves ended
and there I took a taxi to Formentor, a small village on the farthest
point of the island, where I would take the train to Palma
because the bus wouldn't pass through Deyá again
                            for another three days.
"In Formentor there are documents" Graves told me
"that Columbus was born there. I've seen them."
I traveled along a road of endless curves gazing out
as from a plane at a sapphire sea with tiny
little waves and some immense rocks almost like
columns, in the middle of the sea surrounded by surf, and one
or two triangular sails far off . . . The Mediterranean
                    "with its iodine breath and saline scent"
as Rubén said here.

The car arrived at Formentor just in time to catch
the train to Palma de Majorca from where I'd later

leave for Barcelona and from there to Italy alongside that
sea of Venus and of Homer, of Ulysses and the sirens
and the White Goddess.

With the Lapps

Korvatonturi
the mountain where Santa Claus lives
(children are answered from the Helsinki mail office)
and I walked close to
        the Arctic Polar Circle
land full of tiny Christmas trees
        invited by the lady minister of culture
        me a minister too in those days
        to see the midnight sun
        June 23rd.
The northernmost place in Finland
where you can go by plane
and then by car
and then over a silver lake
with no inhabitants
        to the meeting place
        of Lapps with their reindeer.
The lake turned silver by the eight p.m. sun
like the 3 p.m. sun in my country.
        The blue sky seemed lower
        and the clouds in it lower
        than in my country.
        And the mosquitoes!
No comparison
        between the mosquitoes of the tropics
        in quantity and voracity
and those of the arctic!

                On a high rock
                        the solitary silhouette
                        of a reindeer.

The Lapps
have 1,000 words for the reindeer
        male reindeer, small reindeer

small male reindeer, small female reindeer
but in Finnish there are only 10.

The midnight sun
              or the night without darkness.
This is the day of 24 hours of light
              (at the pole it's 6 months)
and the day for the reindeer gathering
in an immense uninhabited area
to be marked by their owners
the ones born that year.
                            With a small light aircraft
                            the reindeers rounded up.

The reindeers with their branches
their antlers
              as though with dry sticks on their heads.
The reindeers gathered in the corral
                            running around
horns clashing against horns
in the tight herd
              all with the gentle bleat of children
and the small ones in that tumult
              losing their mothers
and finding them again
                            identifying their scent
and losing them again.

Infinite vastness of tiny conifers
of a sad green
in the melancholy light of dusk.
              But the Lapps wearing colorful clothes
                            the children like princes.

They had put up a reindeer-skin tent
for us to spend the night
              the earth floor covered in brushwood.
              Outside a campfire

over which we roasted pieces of reindeer
threaded on spruce skewers
and which we ate burning our hands.
An old Lapp
like a Miskito Indian
told the minister she told me
that he wanted to sleep with her
(he didn't know she was a minister).

     The red sun did not sink
     totally
       on the horizon.

We were drinking an alcoholic beverage
I don't know what it was.
No ideas but in things
William C. Williams used to say.
  From the trip to that day without night
  these are the things.

Tata Vasco

In case you didn't know
Sir Thomas More's island Utopia
was Cuba.
An island "in the shape of a crescent moon"
the Chancellor of England describes it
     and the sea calm as a lake.
The island of Columbus and Pedro Mártir and Fidel Castro.
"In truth they maintain
that the land like the sun and the water belongs to all"
says Pedro Mártir
         and without *mine* and *yours*.
        A communism on the island which now is Cuba.
Your infinite island Cintio Vitier
("They told Columbus that it was an infinite land
of which no one had seen the end
           although it was an island")
Utopia is not an imaginary island but in the Antilles.
Nor like something from Jules Verne or H. G. Wells.
It was not a fantasy of More's says Martínez Estrada.
And Pedro Mártir:
     "For them it is the Golden Age
they do not enclose their lands
without laws, without books, without judges
they cultivate maize, yucca, yam like on Hispaniola"

Through Pedro Mártir and Vespucci
More came to know of it.
     The new world had no name
        Atlantis? The Fortunate Isles? Paradise?
They gave it Vespucci's name
Because it had no name
          and still has none.
To Columbus Cuba was China and Haiti Japan
he never knew of the New World

he believed his glory was the Passage to the Indies
with no new name to give.

And Amerigo did not discover America but described it.
A thousand leagues to the west of the Canary Isles:
      "They go about completely naked
      "their hair long and black especially the women
      "they swim like fish and the women better than the men
      "they have no chiefs nor war leaders
      "each one lord of himself
      "they do not quarrel among themselves and speak softly
      "there is no marriage and they go with whom they please
          "they are not ashamed of their private parts
          "their houses are cabins and they live in community
          "their riches are feathers of many-colored birds
          "and tiny green and white pebbles
          "but they show no interest in pearls and gold

And Don Vasco de Quiroga (*Tata Vasco*)
came to Mexico as Judge [magistrate]
of his Majesty the Emperor Carlos V
barely 10 years after the fall of Tenochtitlán
      —and later bishop of Michoacán—
read More's *Utopia* in México, and took it seriously
and implemented it!
          Two hundred years later his work still existed
and the Indians still remember him as *Tata Vasco*
      (although he is forgotten in his native town
      La Villa Madrigal de las Altas Torres
      in Castilla la Vieja).
His idea a social system for the entire continent
taken from More as he himself says
and from Lucian's *Saturnalia* translated by More and his friend Erasmus
      (and by what Pedro Mártir wrote about Cuba)

Extraordinary that a lawyer and later bishop
fifteen years after the publication of More's *Utopia*

written as a joke according to Chesterton
should dare to implement it among the Mexican Indians.

The plan of a Republic
                for all the Indians of the New World.

The Utopians (according to More)
        everything being held in common wanted for nothing
        which is why poor people or beggars were unknown
        and its inhabitants are rich although they own nothing
        with such equality that all live in abundance
        Agriculture learnt from childhood
                        Six hours work each day
                Always the same clothes and they don't change fashion
                There was no money
                                They detest war
        The island of Utopia without private property

                Utopia of the holy Chancellor of England . . .
Who hid a hair shirt under the gold chains
and only removed it before dying in the Tower of London.
        Great friend of More's was Erasmus.
        And also the King.
The King strolls for an hour on the banks of the Thames
with his beloved Thomas More
the royal arm around his neck
                        the neck that he would behead.
        (More had said to his wife
        that the King loves him greatly
        but for a castle in France
        would give his head)

But More's imaginary utopia
        in Quiroga was a Magna Carta for America.
The happy society of the Indians
                according to the model of the beheaded Chancellor.
To Quiroga More was not
a theoretical rambling but an immediate application.

                    An outstanding achievement says Alfonso Reyes
of implementing "Utopia" among the Mexican Indians.
            "Most simple people of this New World
            so docile and similar to those of the Republic
            of this author Thomas More, a most wise man
            with more than human wit . . ." (Quiroga to the Council of the Indies)

"For which not without great cause this is called the New World
and these its natural people are still in its golden age"

One who reduced to practical terms More's dream.
He put *Utopia* into practice.
                    He found Plato's Republic
                    perfect and compressed in *Utopia*
                    and he tried it in America.
            As in Plato and as in More property held in common.
                        Utopia, island of the ocean sea
                    was dreamt of by a genius
                    and another genius implemented it
Neither More nor Plato ever thought
that their republics would be reality.
But utopia for More in Quiroga was a reality.

A man of the libraries of Europe
he was also a man of action.
Founder of an institution in Mexico
which in More was a fantasy.
He reads More's novel
and its laws should be the laws of the New World.
Magistrate of the crown and after a bishop,
                                who conceived of
adjusting the lives of the Indians to More's scheme.
To elevate the Indians
to a higher level than the European.
            Still in the thick of conquest!

"Most gentle, most meek, most humble people
without pride, ambition nor greed in the least"

Barefoot men with long hair
in the manner used by the apostles
the guests to the huge banquet in the New World!
With vices naturally
but not proud or ambitious
they are content with little and survive on next to nothing
May we never be left with the shame he says
of having laid the land and a new world like this to waste
People so docile and gentle, humble and obedient
of such soft wax as these
for whatever you wish to do with them
Without care or grief for the morrow
with indifference and neglect of finery
barefoot, without handling money among themselves
If More had seen the Indians of Michoacán!

When he arrived they had taken refuge in the mountains
fleeing from the madmen on horseback searching for jewels.
Pátzcuaro razed, the temples of Tzintzuntzán burnt.
The face of the Indians branded with the iron.
The face in the image and likeness of God
with the burning letters of the buyers.
That like flocks of sheep had to be branded.
The poor Indian alone in his hut unarmed and naked . . .
They brought their grievances to him in pictures
and the interpreter wept when he said it in the language of Castile.
He succeeded in getting them to return and rebuild their villages.

"As I have seen that Lucian says in his *Saturnalia*
of those people that they call of gold and golden age
in which there was in all and for all the same equality . . ."
"the men of gold of the golden century of the first age"
"I see in these an image of those from the Golden Age"
"Because it is not in vain but with much cause and reason
it is called the New World not because it was found new
but because it is like that of the first age and of gold"
"in this golden age of this New World"
"as they served each other in the golden first age

similar to that which they now have in this new World"
" . . . in this new world and in my view first age"
(To him the Golden Age was almost natural in the Indies.
      Age of iron that of the Spanish)

He found in the Indians some qualities, a psychology
closer to the Golden Age than the Europeans.
        To Utopia.
Like made of wax . . . To do what he wanted.
      Taking away the bad from them and leaving the good with them
      and converting their good into better.
To create a kind of Christians like the early church.
      Sharing of possessions of the early church
      that Solon, Lycurgus and Plato so desired.
There were no social classes in More's Utopia
      (although there were in Plato's Republic)
Equal each with the others, and the others with the others
        without rich people nor servants
as also in Quiroga.
And the dream of an enormous project of a Christian Arcadia
"in this primitive new Church of this New World"
        "A very large and very reformed church"
The Spanish with the Indians
like Christ to us doing good and not evils.
      And it was precisely in THE DESTRUCTION OF THE INDIES
          that he saw Utopia possible.

From his cell: the children in the mud, bellies swollen.
        Those to whom he is going to teach Latin, etc.
As he also mentions naked natives in the markets
craving the food left by pigs.
      "naked and barefoot, eating grass"
the homeless Tarascans
      to whom he gave houses.
Indians that no one had ever defeated
spontaneously submissive in his presence.
        Not the doing of things for the Indians
        but making the Indians do them.
He did not reject Spaniards in his foundations

(conquistadors and settlers)
And he brought the Indians and the Spanish together in a College
so they would teach each other their languages.

    Superior to that dreamed by More
    what Quiroga achieved.
There was slavery in More's ideal city
But not in Quiroga's royal settlements.
He established the community of property.
Turns at work in the city and in the country.
And also the work of women.
        And the 6-hour working day More stipulates.
Nobody idle and everyone punctual in their occupations
but with nobody killing themselves working
and the free time everyone in their own pursuits.
        (Thus Thomas More in his *Utopia*)
And the State in Utopia according to More
had the aim
of exempting from physical work
the longest time possible.
        (So too in Quiroga)

A system of social happiness
        Avant la lettre
EVERYTHING IS SHARED BETWEEN YOU
ACCORDING TO YOUR CONDITION AND NEED
Work should be tolerable and placid.
The children with their studies and their work in the fields
    "to read, to write and to sing"

He began with 2 dozen Indians, still a Judge
buying land with his own funds
in Tacubaya 2 leagues outside Mexico City
    (now it is part of Mexico City
    and my student lodgings were there)
        And later, a bishop by then, in Michoacán . . .

It was in Michoacán his great work.
In Michoacán More's fantasy made real.

The 54 cities in More's fiction
he sought to found them in Michoacán.
                Adaptation of a utopian dream
                                to practical reality.
As in *Utopia* and in Plato's *Republic*
the land belonging to all and not to individuals.
Each family with its house and plot of land as in the USSR.
Basic unit the family as in More.
                The land of the Tarascans was self-sufficient
                                and prosperous.
                "Nobody suffered want"
which was possible due to the work in common
                "of the said six hours of work in common"
The surplus
for the sick, orphans, widows and the elderly.
Nobody owner of the means of production.
A system of peoples exchanging their industries.
The need that they had some for the others united them.
Through commerce and industry it united them.
                The agricultural work obligatory
                (other occupations chosen freely)
And he created the school allotments.
So they were skilled in agriculture from childhood.
                The people without jails.
Without death penalty. Banishment yes.
They were taught to govern and to obey.
In the lands of New Spain
the way of life of the first Christians.
Where nobody held anything as his own.
                In another of his *Ordinances*:
                                Let there be no beggars or idle friars

More and Quiroga, socialists.
And Quiroga mentions *Saint Thomas More* several times
To the Council of Indies.
July 1535: month of his first document to the Council of Indies
and the month in which More was decapitated.

The first banana in Mexico he planted, Quiroga,
in Tzintzuntzán (brought from Santo Domingo)

and he founded Uruapan with *zapotes, chicozapotes*, limes, lemons
        pines lifted up to the sky
with a beautiful layout and art like a Flemish landscape
     as much cleanliness as could be found in any monastery
and that this is what he knows
       and another witness
has seen them eat like Spaniards in great harmony
According to what this witness has seen
       they seemed more like nuns
(the Tarascan Indians)
         They were not taught Greek but Latin yes
Some speaking it like clerics.
He insisted like More on the clothes
"as you presently use them, of cotton, white, clean, honest"
"Item
they breed many fowl of Castile and of the land"
     Each house with its kitchen garden
"Item the kitchen gardens mentioned above for their recreation"
     The girls work with wool and linen, cotton and silk.
     Males can marry at 14
     Women at 12
They hold parties, banquets and celebrations in common
" . . . a large room where you can eat together to greater cheer"
In his will he orders: "Concede nothing whatsoever."
The work that lasted 200 years.
Which the socialist (or communist?) leader Toledano called
—the dismay of Catholics in my student days in México—
     "a difficult model to surpass."
And he furthermore called it the new Quetzalcoatl.

Still on the islands and the shores of the lake of Pátzcuaro
the Tarascans call him *Tata Vasco*
(*Tata,* father, also applied to God)

     And Tata Vasco the father of Mexican handicrafts.
He not only perfected the Indians' crafts
but introduced new ones.
     Teachers from Spain. The Tarascans learnt everything.
In each town a skill

—as the tourist sees today—
not by chance or because it was always that way but
because 400 years ago
Quiroga planned it.
      Garlands of flowers and birds of the lacquer ware of Pátzcuaro
      inspired by flowers and birds that Quiroga drew.
He became a craftsman who knew about dyes
could decorate like a Chinese worker
teaching how to make guitars and violins
providing the loom and designing fabrics
painting wooden trays.

He discovered the unknown man of Michoacán:
                      the Artist.
      Vast community of craftspeople
      around the lake of Pátzcuaro.
Pátzcuaro with its mosaics of hummingbird feathers
under Quiroga's guidance.
The skills distributed in different towns
in one cotton, in another those with feathers
some in wood, others copper and others silver and gold.
      Painting, sculpture, agriculture, music
with their dedicated populations
      dependent each on the others
and united by mutual commerce and mutual love.
      In abundance all necessities.
The markets on different days and in different towns
so as not to compete.
Frying pans, saucepans, dishes, copper pots
      in Santa Clara de los Cobres.
Wrought iron in San Felipe de los Herreros,
in Paracho guitars, small ones for children
or fine concert ones, and ordinary guitars, merry guitars
from the bullfights and serenades and *mañanitas* of México.
Shoemakers in Teremendo.
Bedspreads and shawls in San Juan de las Colchas.
Ceramics in Tzintzuntzán, Santa Fe de la Laguna, Tiríndaro

(now throughout Mexico)
In Pátzcuaro painting with oils European style.
Uruapan beautiful city like those of Plato:
for this city there was lacquer ware
                    To describe them is to profane them
which we've all seen.
Uruapan ("where the flowers open")
and its lacquer ware, its famous lacquer ware
            plates, fruit bowls, wooden chests, cups
and above all trays
        first the drawing with a knife
        the details next with a bodkin
        the colors rubbed in with the finger
        and *aje* pigment, the insect called *aje*
        with which they painted their cups since ancient times.
The drawings of flowers which the painter was seeing
stylizations of their kitchen gardens
lilies, pansies, daisies, violets, forget-me-nots
every color of petal and green of the flower stems
with black background and blue black, blue, yellow, red, cherry:
colors of *ajes* crushed in oil which never fade.

And Pátzcuaro his favorite, the center of the handicrafts.
Tin musical instruments, *chirimías*,
textiles, silverware, Christs from sugarcane, blown glass
feather mosaics in the museums
            The Michoacán Christ in the Canaries
            "Their curiosities are everywhere"
And the fishing of the white fish of Pátzcuaro
in the islands and the villages of the lake
where they were taught to make nets and dragnets.
Tata Vasco strolls through the market of Pátzcuaro.
He sees the sale of bananas thanks to the banana he brought.
Blankets from San Juan de las Colchas, enamels from Uruapan.
            Pátzcuaro without beggars.
He sees the bartering
            This blanket for your painted cup

                    This fattened hen for a bag of maize
(Don Vasco's bartering persists in Erongarícuaro)

Beautiful lake of Pátzcuaro that I saw
                              sky color
the fisherman in his small canoe
fishing with his double net "butterfly wings"
        in the twilight
                    the dawn pink sky emptied into the water.
It was for the Tarascans "Heaven's Gate"
the place of the entrance to Paradise.
        Or where the gods went up to heaven
                    "which means *Pátzcuaro* among them"
It was Don Vasco's favorite place.
There he founded the city.
        Personally he laid out the streets.

Night is falling.
                The lake full of canoes
        all of them with the two parallel nets
                                        dragonfly wings
        The poetic dragonflies with which they fish.

I look for the last time
        at this lake Pátzcuaro before I die:
painted as though with a paintbrush the sky and the lake
the shores of fragrant woods
and on the leaves the millions of *ajes*
with which they paint flowers and leaves
and on the flowers the birds of their cups
also painted with *aje*
and the Indians singing the canonical hours.

You can still see Don Vasco in the market of Pátzcuaro
with the polychrome ceramics and all kinds of lacquer ware
expensive and cheap and fruits and birds of every color
vegetables of many smells and so many flowers
strident colors of shawls and bedspreads and blankets

and fish.

>White fish of Pátzcuaro
>The shining skin of silver and diamonds
>>in garlic sauce.

More successful than Las Casas.

Quite forgotten now Vasco de Quiroga
but not by the Tarascans.
They still call him *Tata Vasco* in Michoacán.

There is a hole where he left his footprint in the mud
according to legend
and the walker placed his right foot there
so his footprint would not be erased.
>So his footprint would not be erased.

In the Sea of Cortez

It was no longer the whale season
though we had come here for whales
    but we beheld
in the Gulf of California
or Sea of Cortez (which Cortez discovered)
the dolphins
      —as we traveled by boat to the island of Espíritu Santo—
        suddenly the sea filled with curved backs
        with sharp curved fins
            bodies in aerodynamic half-moons
              leaping into the air
fleets of black planes emerging from the sea
               and falling back
      sharp tails and very pointed beaks
    a thousand or so all around us
and amongst them also babies
diving down and surfacing again up ahead
        leaping
           swift and joyful
frolics
      teasing the boat so it seems
their heads turned around to see if we see them
    and bucking and bouncing
          they disappeared

And later, on the island's rocky coast
singing
    or more like the grunting of hogs that song
      a flock of sea
lions singing
raucous
    like cows without legs
      agile in the sapphire liquid
    but clumsy among the rocks
          white with guano

    shining

                              they writhe around plump
            long-mustached and hairless
                    heads huge without necks and without ears
skin a smooth felt pelage it appears to us
            some in the water on their backs
                    or dancing in the water
and on the coast the young sucking on their mothers' milk

Solentiname Notes

I

Day breaks
Grey lake with gentle waves
Three islands
—before me—
hazy in the rain:
the far one grey
grey-green the middle one
the closest one a soft green
A large white heron flies slow
Several black birds flash past

II

Pink white yellow colored clouds
(only slightly hazier
than the ones above)
in the crystal lake

III

The serenity of this
silver and blue lake
silver more than blue
Distant volcanoes a soft blue
Above like snow-clad peaks
or shaving cream:
their reflection in the lake
which makes it silvery

White Holes

Vancouver / fall / 91
satchels, shorts, T-shirts, miniskirts, jeans,
books under arms and notepads and jotters,
soft legs sunning themselves next to hard biceps,
a couple with Cokes and sandwiches on a tray,
other guys and girls reading or writing or doing nothing,
sandals or trainers swift or slow
on the grass, footpaths or steps; fabrics of every color
like the flowers bordering the grass, footpaths and steps.
Flowers! They will soon wither in the fall.
It's the first day of school and the first day of the fall.
        T-shirts, jeans, satchels . . .
to be young again and be here a college student!
I see Rosario Castellanos sitting alone on a bench,
her hair in the same old chignon,
(later she was a Mexican ambassador and died electrocuted)
sipping something with a straw,
seen as in a dream in which she doesn't recognize me.
There are green pines and beyond them the mountains are covered in snow.
This isn't Mexico University nor is it 45 years ago.
We thought we were happy
and we thought that no one would die,
        unless it was somebody with bad luck,
and that none of us would grow old.

The universe is not a meaningless accident,
nor, Rosario, was your death an accident.
There is a mystery at the end of the universe
and you are now within it.
Unless we die others are not born.
And through the death of others we have been born.
Without death there'd be no human species
nor any species.
In other words, there'd be no evolution.
—From the old to the young—.

Without death there'd be no future.
Life would be arrested
at its very inception.

There are those who believe life came from another planet
because vegetation is green.
The leaf rejects green, which catches the eye,
and is the greatest energy of sunlight,
while it absorbs the red which nourishes it less.
And it's because this life came from another sun.
Hoyle believed illnesses were extraterrestrial.
But whatever the case, death came with life.

Do extraterrestrials bury their dead?
The earth will fill up with dead people,
until there's not a square inch without them,
and the dead will say: we thought we were going away
and we would never be together again.

Incidentally, when Alejandro died,
his young son said that Felipe and Donald
and Elbis and Laureano (his martyr companions)
rejoiced and said laughing
"now we are complete again."
Incidentally also
                his mama dreamed he was saying to her
                "mama, I already took the medicine"

To die is to enter into God.
When God is no longer Another but you.
                You are God.

It is union with God now free of religion.

To live is a temporal flux of what is eternally together
where the past has not passed and the future is long gone.

We die because we are in a non-stationary universe.
It's an "age" phenomenon of all star systems.

And life is organization more than substance
according to Dyson and consequently
it may be free of flesh and blood.

        Non-molecular life:
in the final phase of cosmic evolution.
In which, I suppose, neither economics will exist.
Chemistry became biology
four thousand million years ago.
What might biology be one day?

Every species has continued to divide.
Only one has united more and more.
So are we not at the stage
of considering all minds
as part of a single system?

            The tree could grow indefinitely
            but preferred to produce seeds.

Death is recycling.
Death is another phase of life.
The entire planet is recycling, or there'd be no life.
        If not, how?
                    Sacred recycling.
It's entering into new combinations.

There is something which doesn't die in us.
A DNA of the risen bodies . . .
Resurrection is an organic process.
How? Given the cosmos we have
that *how* is not difficult.
A sort of application of the law
of the conservation of energy.

The same force that brought us out of the chaos
is that which carries us towards death.
But what Prigogine says is

that disorder is not the final destination
from which no one escapes, but is where order is born from.
And these particles of life so brief
they almost don't exist, are what create the whole of reality.
And our lives are scarcely a little longer
than virtual particles
but out of them too order emerges.
Mind that understands the cosmos:
a cosmos creator of the mind.
Both things the same thing.
Born from the stars
studying the stars.
The explanation for all this
physicists would like to know.

The anti-entropic birth of the world.
And there's a common cosmology in all the galaxies.
"Stars are social, always in galaxies."
It would appear there are more stars than are needed.
Within them is where matter became light
         —although what light is we don't know—
and among them there are black holes made of nothing
merely our concepts of space and time.
Accumulation of black holes in black space
until nothing is left of the universe, they say,
except the Second Law.
         Progress versus the decadence of the universe.
         Decadence of the universe versus progress.
The battle of the stars lost in advance?
If the universe had a birth it will have a death
there's no turning back the page. And resurrection?
                                        Some think
that at the heart of every galaxy there is a black hole
where the size is zero and the velocity infinite.
                  And galaxies continue to spin
                  towards the fatal common center
                  to die.
But in the black hole matter dies and is reborn.

The black hole is also white hole.
Black hole here and elsewhere white.

The cosmos has been created for the resurrection.
A goal which is not static, naturally.
"Will we defeat the Second Law of Thermodynamics?"
is the cry of all the earth's dead.

Ah, a decomposition as noble as iron's
and not this maggots' nest which made a saint of the Duke of Gandia
when he had to open the queen's coffin.

>That hydrogen when it becomes helium
>should not become entirely helium,
>inert helium, lifeless or deathless
>until the end of the centuries amen,
>and that element 6 should descend
>like a messiah—carbon—
>predestined to produce life,
>practically limitless carbon,
>freed of the limitations
>of the other elements shows
>that life defies the Second Law.

A fundamental principle, or
the fundamental principal:
from two microscopic cells
millions and millions of cells are born
                    and the blue whale dances in the sea.
From the small to the large.
If a molecule was like a car,
they say, a cell would be the Ford company.
>From simplicity to complexity,
>from confusion to organization,
>progression in a single direction.
Consciousness, says Schrödinger,
the plural of which is unknown,
Schrödinger, the greatest demolisher of the concept of matter.

Let's call it dematerialization.
Waves of matter insubstantial
as waves alone without the water.
"What we call matter without understanding it"
And it is not only waves nor only particle
but a confused mixture of the two.
Our body is particle
and our mind is wave.
The mind is relationships
and what it relates to is matter.
The mind is not matter but its relationships
and the difference between our intelligence
and an electron's is a question of degree.
Particle and wave are person and community.
And Bohr's remark: "With atoms words
can only be used as in poetry."
Just as there is no distance between things,
and nothing is solid, and the separation is not real.
Jazz which improvises as it goes along,
nobody knowing where it will end.

We grow old and die like automobiles.
But if time doesn't exist nobody has died.
So that things don't all happen together
that's time, Wheeler says.
Everything is simultaneous. Time
makes it appear non-simultaneous.
"Time . . . you who do not exist"
You who do not exist except in my neurons.
Turned out there's no separation between living creatures
nor space nor time which separates. And Einstein
who said that this was phantasmal and absurd
got it wrong.
All those we call dead are alive
because the past exists like the present
although unseen.
And when they wash Che's face
he becomes a kind of Christ.

"Che never spoke much about Che"
says his daughter Hilda.

Seems now that, like space and time,
life is also inherent to the universe.
The entire cosmos could be a black hole
and we are all tumbling into that hole
but so as to emerge in another reality
in a white hole.

Day will come when the sea will boil
and the earth's crust will melt
along with all the dead it once held.
The sun will grow and draw close to the earth
and will explode with a light they'll see
millions of light years from here,
and all the dead will go in that light.
Fear of death is an optical error.
That starry sky, what does it tell us?
That we're part of something much larger.
Individual eternity like
part of a community of eternities. And
individual consciousness which emerges
and is diluted in the universal.
        Ontologically together.
        The union of the universe.

Just as we see only the visible part of the spectrum,
which we call light,
so we see only the here and now, and the rest
is in deep darkness.
        (Death for example)

        We are like someone traveling on a train
        seeing everything that passes
        but not what lies ahead.

        The leaves are alive, and
        the flowers of course,

but not the whole tree,
its bark is dead:
they are my dead ancestors,
death in the living tree.

The bird is born with living feathers
which by the time it flies are dead
and it's in order to fly they died.

The study of fossils demonstrates
that species never repeat themselves,
and the life is new each time. Death
therefore necessary. Alejandro, Laureano,
there'll be other yous who will come after.
                    There'll be other Camilos, said Fidel.

In the final Revolution the dead
will all be resurrected.

"The sacred cornfield" say present-day Mayas
                    (the dead)

Everything is evolution. That's to say
everything serves everything.
Single-celled creatures don't die
because they are only single-celled.
                    And neither do they evolve.
Mejía Sánchez when he got a little tipsy would say,
making us all laugh:
"We are almost happy."
A little sad that jokey *almost*
in front of happy.
But now that you've died Mejía
I tell you "you almost died."

Consciousness is different from matter and therefore
can survive the body.
                    Death will die.

The most universal law:
everything is born and dies in the universe,
even the stars.
What will be born of this universe?

The parish priest of São Felix de Marinha (Portugal) preaches
not to place flowers on graves, nor keep them tidy.
All the graves are empty.
When he goes to his village he doesn't visit his parents' grave.
There's nobody in cemeteries, he says.

As a peasant, Alejandro knew every tree.
Commenting on the Gospel in the church in Solentiname
he said: "Many of the roof supports here are madrone trees,
but they don't have white blossom as they did in the wild
in December, because now they're something else.
Now they're well painted and will last many years.
But this change is painful. We are madrone trees . . ."
and he'd painted these supports in cheerful colors.
Without a scaffold, perched on them (I was afraid he'd fall).
        Green, blue, pink, those madrone trees.
He's buried there with his martyr companions
under Sandino's red and black flag
which is red over black—Sandino said—because
black is death and red is resurrection.

                We were talking about black holes . . .
                        Infernal black holes.
We were in Albaicín with Luis García Montero
and his daughter asked, when he said
that a girl her age had been burned alive: "Why?"
"Because the house caught fire." "Why?"
"Because her parents weren't there." "Why?"
"Because they'd gone out and the firemen arrived
but too late." "Why?" Luis doesn't answer this.
I tell them: "This is the *why*
humanity has been asking forever."
"Since it was a little child like you, Irene" says Luis.

I say St. Augustine asked it and came up with nonsense.
Such as newborn babies went to hell.
Job asked it and God answered (not very convincing).
And that WHY? in Aramaic. "Father, why have you . . ."
                    A God of necessity and chance.
                    And therefore variable, not immutable.
What's at stake is not the divinity of Jesus
says Miranda, but the divinity of God.
Bearing in mind that
in the first century of our Christian
era which is or was our era
God destroyed the religious image of God.
He ate and drank with us, shat and pissed.
Luther clarified that God's right hand is everywhere.
Which is why there's the Transcendence of Nicaragua and Nigeria.
The resurrection is not individual but collective.
And all the extraterrestrials in which he has become flesh
are together with us the body of Christ.
He's the Head, and he's the reason for the cult of skulls.
The only one who can save us from entropy.
He didn't come to explain pain but to share it.
He taught us to mutter *Abba.*   And to say *Okay*
a word not from English but from the Idaho Indians.

The universe is not just stranger than we supposed,
says Aldane, but stranger than we could ever suppose.
Black holes are dimensionless matter.
And white ones?
"Behold I fill the cosmos with white holes."
The dead will recover their dimension.
                    So let's say O.K.

The Caves

Already in the Higher Pleistocene
symmetry, line, color were known.
And the painter has endured 30,000 years.

Delicate doe merely with straight lines.
The head two lines at right angle,
the body a triangle, and the loooong back
a line curved at the end like a hind leg.
Modern art traveled 20,000 years back in time.
In Font de Gaume the two reindeer now faint,
        behind the curtain of calcite,
the female crouched its legs bent,
the male in front with large antlers
gently licking her forehead.
        Not a hunting scene.

In the ice age there was no art for art's sake,
rather a common origin of religion and art.
        Those frescoes are religious.

Neither good lighting nor close to the entrance,
but deep inside in dark and secret chambers.
The "Black Chamber" of Niaux, 800 meters inside the earth,
Trois-Frères: half an hour of mysterious passageways.
And in Cabrerets, hours of labyrinths.
        Lascaux with its incredibly narrow entrance:
        and no remains reveal it was used as dwelling;
                but in the clay dances.
Marsoulas: millennia after being inhabited
those caves were painted.
        Also Altamira when it was no longer occupied.
Paintings to be viewed only by torchlight.
In inaccessible places. Or in hiding places. Or narrow niches.
        Initiations? In Tuc d'Audobert
you cross the underground river,
then the almost vertical slope,

and the interminable labyrinths, difficult passages,
till finally you arrive at the awesome sight
                                (emotion of the initiated!).
Such uncomfortable positions for viewing them.
Paintings upon paintings beneath paintings.
                        Jumble of lines and colors.
Art which existed for 500 centuries according to Herbert Kühn.

Merton didn't believe that they were
magical commercial adverts for bison meat.
            Art as contact with mystery,
            or the veiled forces of nature.
            Hidden fount of fertility and life.

In Trois-Frères the dancer with bison hide,
and the flute. Also called the man with the flute.
Behind the animals (charming them?).
And horns like Pan's. Pan is Paleolithic, it seems.
Religion which was then the true religion
and truly the only religion.
                        Paleolithic prayer painting
                        and music and song and dance.
                        And something more intangible which leaves no trace.
His name? We don't know. Nor if he had a name.
        (Perhaps very imprecise attributes).
But Lissner finds
no evolution of the idea of God. It was already there
when the biped began to think.

Luminous cathedrals within the earth
pre-Reims, pre-Chartres.
                        Ice age liturgies.
                        Pictorial mysticism?
                        Contemplation-Painting?
In Niaux the doorway is scarcely a crevice
and inside so huge. Beyond a narrow passageway

the silent colossalness. Where the floor absorbs the footsteps.
        Mysticism is prehistoric.

        Lord of the Animals?
        Lady of the Animals?
        Supreme Male or Female Being.

Plastic prayers for fertility and life.
        Deep inside, where you have the two bison.
        The male about to fuck the female.
And the little clay phalluses, and footprints
of adolescents in the direction of those phalluses.
Ritual procession towards the copulation of the bison.

Perhaps an initiation with fertility rites.
        Or fertility rites at any rate.
There are bone flutes in the caves, that's to say music,
and in the mud the tracks of the dance to that music.

Rites turned red by the torches.
There are indications of sacrificial meals.
Eucharist in those cave-sanctuaries.
The oldest altars on earth.
The bears are well ordered, bear skulls.
Few stone tools—no sign
of them being made inside the cave.
Far from any water. Not dwellings: sanctuaries.

        One man on his own was not enough.
There must have been a group of illuminators
                        (priests, or at least initiates)
with lamps of hollyhock wick and tallow
which was like having the sun in the cave.
And he in front of the wall with his earth colors,
ochres, hematites, manganese dioxide.
        Black, red, yellow.
Red outlines of the bison.
Tense deer. Hairy mammoths. Horses galloping.

Earth colors under the earth.
Picasso, Miró in those caves.
Manganese oxide the black.
Iron oxide the red.
Calcium carbonate the white.

Fixed with lime water from the caves.
Paul Klee, Chagal.
In profile generally. Horse, bison, antelope.
Superimposed many times on a different scale.
Over horse head a deer with huge antlers.
Without central figures. Animals sometimes upside down.
Huge bison with dainty ladies' feet.
30,000 years without evolution in the art.
As though they leapt forth from the walls.
Luminous, running off into the dark.
Symbols and animals.
Animals that are symbols
and the symbols animals.
The animal-symbol on the rock.
No reason to draw a distinction.
The painted animal and the one outside
weren't they the same animal?
The mammoth was of rock
and the rock was mammoth
in a world in which all was one.

The modern artist plunged into the deepest part of his ego
as labyrinthine as the cave depths.

Where you find the Dordogne bison, with his back
which is the natural stone itself.
The artificial natural.
Since conscious and unconscious they painted together.
And within and without were the same.

Outside the bull lowered its head forming an arc
which was a mere second in the bull's movements

but on the cave wall the arc remained eternal.
The reindeer's leap frozen in the rock
and 30,000 years later it is motionless.

That age-old dialogue with eternity.
And with the day-to-day.
Engraved on a deer horn
horses and fish
(could be colts crossing a river in springtime
when the salmon were rising).
Now there's needle, thread and clothes from hides.
The climate was as it is now in Siberia.
A fiery animal was subjugated, the horse.
"Laurel leaf" knives. There are some so delicate
they could only be ceremonial or symbolic.

They lived in a world of total mystery.
Why did the sun appear and disappear every day?
And up above every night sort of coals lit up.

At the start of the Mousterian the belief
in life after death was already there.

Of the Megaliths we know nothing.
Only that community existed.

Altamira fascinates us
though we don't understand it.

And we're the same.
We're the same as the cave people
those nowadays called civilized.
Biologically we're the same.

Abstraction was already there in the Aurignac age.
And abstract art together with the realism of the bison.
Paleolithic abstract and still more in the Neolithic.
To render visible the invisible, say the unsayable.

Animals don't know symbols: they are symbol.
And between them and the hunter there is an abyss.

We know nothing of what was dreamed of in those caves
but those caves are in our dreams.

The harpoon inside the body like in X-rays,
as though seen in X-ray. Lascaux: the viscera hanging out.
In Trois-Frères a bear bristling with arrows. What is it?
                    There are altars, it seems.

Cave god of the cave man.
That liturgy is now so far away from us.

The little Mayerdof reindeer sacrificed in May
(May according to the antlers) at the start of the hunt.
          Everything they painted was sacred.
          Or there was no profane and sacred.

Painting images in caves
he imagined he was in God's image,
and kneading little clay figures
kneaded by the hands of God.

          The chapel of the Madeleine is small.
          Females pursued by males
          or mounted by males, or pregnant females.
The polychrome backs of Altamira,
only the rock with color.
Animal-line-rock-animal one and the same.
          Below the valley with mountain goats
          and the stream with salmon rising.

Still no awareness of an individual soul but collective?
Still without individual identity but of the species?
Therefore without death. The individual dies, not the species.
          Beings without ego were they?
          Even in the *Iliad* there are no individualities.
It appears they lived without past or future.

Without time. They just lived.
Without time. Not without moon.
      The moon showed them life was cyclical.
It dies and is reborn.
      (It would disappear for three days).

      And grass is born, dies and is born again.
It means, they never knew personal death.
And the fact of the earth revolving on its axis,
      half day, half night,
               sleeping, waking,
the birds singing again:
it also created the conviction of the resurrection.

Signs of fires to warm the dead,
according to Spy.
      Understanding it as a continuation of life.
Same as us.
Yes, the Neanderthals too. Slandered Neanderthals.
Slandered too in *Cosmic Canticle*. Thick-lipped,
huge square eye sockets, sunken forehead, no chin:
      But with a cult to the Neanderthal God
(just as there was the Pithecanthropus God and the Sinanthropus God)
and burial rites for Neanderthal children.
      Sacro Pastore, close to Rome, San Felice Circeo:
      occipital orifice artificially enlarged,
      or ringed by stone circles.
And dead buried with flowers
(much pollen on the fossils:
hyacinth, hollyhock, horsetail . . .
—in spring). Which points to
another world, another life, or who knows what beyond,
beyond, naturally, for fuck's sake, death.

      And the sleeping position.
         Death as sleep is prehistoric.

Le Moustier: a child with a small stone pillow.
La Ferrasie: oriented towards the setting sun.

In the Tyrol the bears.
Bear skulls towards the setting sun.
Not through any flood but the hand of man.
No food leftovers: the bones are intact.
And laid out respectfully.
  And in the most inaccessible part of the cave.
    Cave man
    and cave prayer.

And cave man and woman.
Let's define that age:
  a desire for fertility and immortality.
    (One and the same thing)
And in damp clay in the damp caves
in great abundance: Woman.
   A harmony of curves and roundnesses.
Roundnesses of the thighs and the buttocks and the abdomen.
  Between the thighs is the triangle.
An emphasis on the female sex in the Magdalenian.
Sometimes in naturalistic bodies, the vulva
is an abstract triangle.
Or sometimes only the triangle worked over.
Sometimes there are no hands nor feet
but the triangle very detailed
and its size exaggerated.
  The cave was the Mother.
The vulva of our sacred Mother Earth.
Earth from which we came and where we return.

  The *réalité cosmique* according to Eliade.
    To the vulva we return to be born again.
Sacred triangle of the Pythagoreans.
For this reason the most perfect form was the triangle
for the Pythagoreans.
Sometimes only a curved nose and eyebrows
but breasts and buttocks well developed.
  The vulva, the phallus, the breasts.

Sacred sex or sacrament.
Not prehistoric pornography.
And sometimes then mere abstraction.
                           Delta.
And source of all the rivers on earth.
The sacred rivers of Mesopotamia
had their primary source in the vagina of the earth.

A society without economy, or against economy,
in other words without poverty.
                           And without property.
        Nomads, riches would have been a hindrance.
        Nobody with property, and therefore free.
        Without property and therefore without theft and wars.
Later the first riches and the first swords.
But in the Neolithic excavations
        complete absence of weapons.
And in the cave paintings there are no battles.

There was love then, solidarity, compassion.
For there are fossils of handicapped.

The entire Paleolithic was peaceful.
And peaceful even the Neolithic.
The Neolithic village, peaceful.
Peaceful the stone age.
Swords appear with bronze
and ever since there has been no peace.
The ability to store created inequality.
What we have still been unable to suppress.

                  And then shortly afterwards slavery.
In simians it's frequent for there to be a despot.
And the rest docile.
                  They don't flee to form another group,
                      create another party.
But in humans tyranny was greater.

And the subjection (slaves) greater
than that of the most submissive monkey.

In the bison chamber, the last chamber,
the imprinted tracks of the last dance,
in the mud at the end of the Magdalenian.
By the side—abandoned—a flint knife.
They danced the bison's dance and never returned.
The stalagmites and stalactites slowly
dripping for centuries sealing the final chamber.
The chamber of a fertility rite
in which the male bison is behind the female
                    poised to leap to mount her.

A fantasy world under the earth.
And what myths or beliefs or gods
those animals were, we'll never know.

At the end of the ice age that art ceased.
The cave of the paintings closed. Thus it remained
for 15,000 years, until in 1895
four children playing entered it.

Ecce Homo

It is not that man was once there
       (Genesis would be anti-evolutionary)
rather that before man, paradise already existed.
      Ireneus saw it as a *lost change*.
           A paradise in perspective!
Could be we weren't able to enter it.
The first hominids
               (with luxuriant tropical forest)
remained on the threshold.
All primitivism is a first innocence,
like that of childhood,
and a nakedness.
      Isaiah. Oseah, Zachariah,
prophesy the paradise in the future.
We sin in Adam says St. Paul. The hominids.
Fact is there was a freedom. Which was used.
But in Malmö with Daisy I saw the long pier
in a May blue Baltic
and swans in the sea, seaweed in the water, and at the pier end
two strictly separate platforms,
one for the naked men sunbathing,
on the other the naked women
and only the children swimming unseen could see them
raising their little heads out of the water like fish,
although fish are naked too and not ashamed:
Why did nudity provoke "shame"
There's not a theologian or scientist who can say.

Why don't we go around naked,
why striptease, porn mags, Rio Carnival,
nightmares about being naked in the street.
Neither does the Genesis passage explain it.
Palm trees and herons are they naked?
But the woman under the palm tree is naked.
The nakedness in Genesis yet to be interpreted.
        They felt themselves naked? So what . . . !

Could original sin be the reason we wear clothes?
On the shore of Lake Turkana they found
amongst hominid fossils
                    a fossilized fig leaf!
molded in the now petrified mud
a fig leaf.

They say we ceased to have hair like monkeys
to be cooler beneath the tropical sun
and that's when we felt naked.
And black pigments were a modesty of the skin.

But whatever the case
Genesis does not contradict *The Origin of Species*
since paradise
                    is not origin but goal.
                            Original goal, let's say.

The planet was covered with stones
and a hominid used them.
          Flint on flint
          and the arrowhead emerges.
                    Two arrowheads: one shaped inside the brain,
                    the other still shapeless within the flint.
The flint blade replaces tusk blade.
But the most decisive factor in the evolution
of *Homo habilis* wasn't the perfection of tools.
Many animals hunt together
but they don't share the prey.
When the monkey shared food
it was no longer monkey but human.
          Giving and receiving: another thing which made us human.
"The survival of the fittest."
But the fittest show the most solidarity.
Communion rather than combat, says Gould.

No law of the jungle
in those jungles.

The only animal in upright position.
The arms shortened
and the legs grew longer.
There was a physical ability to walk on two legs
and a "biped ideology."
Standing upright made us intelligent,
no longer a brain hanging from a body,
but on top of a vertical spine dominating it all.
So it became larger
and with increased forehead.
4 times larger than the monkey's
which is why the forehead bulged outwards.
                    The hand no longer walked.

The longer he was upright
the more he used his hands.
The more he used his hands
the longer he was upright.

Fire also served to bring us together.
Fire was language, stories.
The penultimate little branch of evolution
the Neanderthals.
                    We the last (to date).
        The baby's tiny gripping hand
            is on account of the mother's hairy pelt.
Neanderthal physically outstripped *sapiens*
but never developed the frontal lobes
(those of the imagination and ethics, and also the emotions).

The only vertebrate that was a philosopher.
        The tail had long ceased to serve a purpose.
Fire wasn't only useful but fascinating.
And still is. Children with matches!
Adults in front of the flames in the fireplace.

We brought fire into the cave and we were human.
From within the forest—some burning tree.
We brought the sun into the cave and danced around it.

"As though a strange force chose a fortunate species."
Mankind is group.
Man only exists as a human community.
While dolphins remained frustrated.
Aerodynamic, so without hand right or left.
And in the water, unable to light fire.

The instinct in children to climb trees . . .
It's still unknown why we stood up on two feet.
But standing upright compromised us with the ground,
to become once and for all exclusively terrestrial.

The fingers could move separately,
and thumb and index finger make a circle.
The eyes had been for the night and were large.
Then they were for the day but remained large
but now colors could be seen.
Which was an advantage in the monochrome forest:
a colorful three-dimensional and touchable world,
where you could recognize fruit, grasp it and pick it
      —and give it.
             Separating the concrete from its surroundings.
             That was already thought. And language.
So seeing in colors we owe to the ripe fruits.

The backward curve on the lumbar
made the body erect and also more beautiful.
Maybe that was when they felt naked.
The sex in the middle of their bodies.
      The fruit of ethical knowledge was tasty.
         Eden was in Africa.
Homo erectus: when we became men and no longer monkeys.
Hunter-gatherers, tools, fire.
Paradise wasn't given but offered.

To man and not to the animal. Paradise was the progress
not offered to the animal.

For eons they gazed at the stars
with some regularity and many irregularities
and asked themselves: What are they?
Later they learned arithmetic counting sheep,
        arithmetic which led them to count galaxies.

The only animal with buttocks.
And in upright position his anus was hidden.
Woman the only mammal with permanent breasts,
and the only female with orgasm, and in heat the year round.
So there'd be in those caves an everlasting love.

The only animal that smiles.
Lips modified to be able to smile.
Separated from the gums, and so able to smile.
Also the nose grew longer,
the chin too (both things for speech).
The eye teeth atrophied
which altered our faces and made us talk.
A shorter tongue than in monkeys,
that too was for talking.
First individual symbolic sounds,
then there were general ones for the whole group.
Spending much time together in the cave
increased communication.

The less-human monkeys vanished into the forest.
Did language make us human
or did the human brain make language?
They began to have ideas, notions, death for example.
The only animal that knows he's going to die.
At first language was for practical purposes,
but then it went on to myth and spiritual matters.
"Kidneys no longer just to make urine
but also philosophers."

He domesticated plants and animals
but before that he domesticated himself.

The only animal to wear clothes.
Are clothes to hide the animality?
    Hairless except for the head,
    because of the sun,
    and the sex, to make it stand out.
The buttocks close together with the anus unseen.
Homo sapiens' beautiful eyes, lips, teeth.
Evolution of a species to dominate evolution.
Another difference from animals: we accept responsibilities.
Another difference too:
    that we serve a cause or someone.
"A little less than the angels . . . " says the Psalm.
But why with farts and a rectum?
Their fossils are barely distinguishable from other animal fossils.
    Homo sapiens—Ecce homo
Where God became flesh. What astounded Tertullian:
God born into the world through some shameful parts
and fed in a ridiculous manner?

Every evolutionary change was for survival.
Until us.
And as we're the most adaptable of species
mightn't we adapt beyond death too?
It's easy enough to imagine:
        A collective consciousness
        whose body is the universe.
He knows he's going to die. To be reborn. But to die.

The only animal to cry when it is born.

Gazing at the Stars with Martí

Born from such an improbable event as
the Big Bang.
Before which there was no light, nor darkness either
and neither time
and with which evolution began.
God must have seen that "all was good"
                     billions of years later.
     Life engenders life, but before
non-life engendered life.
Through errors in DNA, variation, evolution.
If it had always been perfect
there'd have been nothing but microbes.
     From amoeba to reptile to apes etc.
     degrees of perceiving more and more reality.
DNA
     all written in the same language and the same alphabet.
     (could there be other languages, other letters on other planets?)
Reptiles' scales were feathers of baby dinosaurs
and later birds. Blind natural selection?
On the other hand there are crustaceans
which in 300 million years have not evolved.
The technology of the spider web is always the same.
     We
     unconscious agents of evolution's acceleration
Not biological, let's be clear.
          That vastness of the universe
          which knows only through us.
          We are intelligent atoms.
          Stars studying the stars.
In the Earth's quagmires the cosmos came alive.
And shortly after—through us—understood itself.
We
     "the most complex of molecules"

     The moon like a rugby ball.
          At 8 a.m. over the Alps.

All that You touch is so beautiful!
What does the earth look like from the moon?
The astronaut replied:—"Fragile."
Neither can you see any division of nations.
And the sun: its white light in the black sky.
From purely chemical reactions
intelligent life here transpired.
Could there be others like this on other planets? With bodies?
Where might evolution have already taken them?
Some could be merely interstellar cloud.
Or intelligent beings composed only of radiation.
Which in our lexis we might call angels.
We're not thinking of Hollywood films.
The meeting would be another step in evolution.
Extraterrestrials and terrestrials.
Then it wouldn't be change but transformation.
After the meeting nothing but a case of working together.
Children from the same womb of the Big Bang.

Three hundred light years away?
                    Three thousand light years?
The "conversation" is not easy.
              The most powerful transmission
would be a faint murmur across the Galaxy.
        Hoping they'll be merciful with us.
Although still no signs of civilization in the neighborhood.
But Lucretius had already thought:
other earths must exist in the heavens with people and animals.
        Why not? Billions of human planets in the Galaxy
In the USSR it was Leninist dogma.
              What impact on our art?
What would another intelligent species be like?
Dyson fears a technology run amok.
And what if all the universe's extraterrestrials, us included,
are trying to build a better universe,
a new universe?

        Metrodorus of Chios wrote:
"A single world with life in the universe would be

like a single ear of wheat in a field."
        (Contrary to Aristotle and the Church.)
If the sun is an ordinary star,
and planets are common to stars
and the chemistry of our bodies . . .
Other Christs in multitudes of planets Descartes believed.
Marconi thought he heard signals from Mars, which must have been
a nearby elevator or thunder in the distance.
But what if the universe is not a single ear
but an entire wheat field?

Solentiname. Ground constellated with fireflies
and sky with millions of nuclear reactions.
I raised up a tiny esparto-grass seed
From the esparto-grass that covers the entire meadow
and I understood the unimportance of size.

Such tiny little stars
which are such huge suns.
What a world you were born into
        Ernestito Laureano
with the big so small
and the small so big.

I lifted up a seed from the flame tree
I sowed here years ago in Solentiname
and in the seed I saw a future flower,
and in that flower a seed and in it
another flower with seed and in the seed another flower,
blood red flame tree after flame tree
flame trees and flame trees and girls
under flame trees or with flame tree flowers in their hair
in the flame tree seed I picked up today.

Universe! Nothing fills me with greater passion than your evolution!
        For millennia *Homo sapiens*
        men and women *Homo sapiens*

have gazed at that beauty up above
without understanding it.
Heavenly we call them and they are
earth and stone like us.
We revolving around one
of the 10^{11} stars in the galaxy.
Beings who defecate, use deodorants,
discovering the secrets of the cosmos.
Which exists through us. It
needed us to be real.

Biological evolution
in the direction of the soul.
Nerve fibers that don't think
are what produce thought.

New means something
which didn't have to be like that.

Evolution is everything that exists.
And it has a purpose. Not just
unpredictable natural selection.
Who wove me within my mother's womb?
The eye perfects itself
until the fetus is ready to emerge.
Without sea water we can't see
and we moisten our eyes with our eyelids
without darkness when we blink.
Electricity and magnetism
is electromagnetism Maxwell discovered, and it's light.
Our eyes are for seeing the light
as far as the origins of time
and beyond the origins: eternity
our future!
Photons are social,
each one makes its own way

but once they arrive it's all together
                              (like us)

There are oceans and lakes up above.
And species already closer to the Kingdom of Heaven?

Blue and white little ball in the black sky
out of the atmosphere.
                         Astral space
that is where we are.
We're the Martians who have already landed.

Time. Time.
Our enemy time!
But creation moves within it and without it
there'd be no evolution
4,000 million years ago we were nothing but rock.
Stone became living beings
which went back to being stone.
                    "It's hard for geologists to find rocks
                         which haven't been part of living organisms"
and we'll return to the depths of the earth
where stone is turned to fire
eventually to emerge as lava
and be living beings once more.
Liquid it emerged from the earth's magma
                    hurled through the mouth of a volcano
           still burning red hot
                                   river of red rock
                 hurtling downhill
molten mass of sodium and silica
and gradually it cooled, solidifying and crystallizing
          separated then from the rest of the mass
                         it was once under the sea
the sea withdrew and rivers swept it along
                                   on it rumbled over the land
              finally coming to rest on a plain

being worn down gradually
by the rain, the sun and the wind
     making it smooth and almost round
               increasingly smaller in size
until one wet September morning
when the filibusters were attacking San Jacinto
Andrés Castro picked it up from the ground
and killed a Yankee with it.

Confucius said:
"Human beings have a single nature.
Their customs (their cultures) separate them."

It's true what St. Augustine says:
we're born between piss and shit.
But here where you see me I'm an extraterrestrial
with particles which were once light years
apart.
Mammal of the order of primates
in His image and likeness in the Quaternary.
From the earth's clay means
from the dust of stars.
We all sinned in Adam means
in *Homo erectus*. Sin is genetic.
Because of fruit colors our color vision.
Eve was black, in sub-Saharan Africa,
with a long, smooth, elegant skull.
She ate berries amid giraffes and gazelles.
          Evolution conscious of itself.
          Conscious of its own evolution.
Reptiles don't dream, they say,
only birds and mammals,
but they live as in a dream.
And when we dream our reptile
ancestors live again in us.

Despite natural disasters
which only religion and insurance companies understand

our social progress corresponds
to an increase in cerebral convolutions.
                    A part of our being which is collective.
Cooperation is at every biological level and
is as old as life.
"I know of no organism that can exist in isolation."
And:
            "To ask about the origins of cooperation
            is like asking about the origins of life."
                    Or in baseball for example.
Individual cells of Myxobacteria, for example,
go out to hunt in groups,
like a pride of lions cornering a gazelle.
Compassion as a factor in evolution.
            Self-sacrifice the other.
Since we were tiny little animals among dinosaurs.
The first economy was sharing.
In this class of planet, this biosphere,
it's cooperation, says L. Thomas.
            What sociobiology demonstrates:
            Doing good to others is doing good to oneself.
"Together we grow, to an even height like a field of corn"
say the Tzotziles of Chiapas.
A myth of our day and age:
that war is in the genes.
We say: we're a cooperative animal.
                    Or that's the hypothesis.

That your picnic may not deprive others of food.
                    To enjoy the planet in equal shares.
The thrush which, confronted by the sparrow-hawk, whistled to
                                    alert the others
would have done better to keep quiet . . .
Muggeridge asked O. Wilson
whether biology could explain Mother Teresa.

Animals have a species-soul.
Which guides the migration of birds.

And in humans the same thing too
but personal.
The language of bees is millions of years old.
yet no one amongst us any longer speaks Sumerian.
And biological evolution has been slowing down
since the Cambrian.

                                 Biological I said.

      According to fossils
       entropy triumphs over biological evolution.
Until one day there'll be no more biological evolution,
merely a human evolution
not biological.

                     I'm twenty years old said Laureano
and I don't want to see the Kingdom of Heaven when I'm an old man
but now.
      (My revolutionary action
       based on faith in the resurrection of the dead
               said the French communist
               expelled from the party).
"love, or rather God"
      Sandino wrote.
"The communism of love"
      (A. C. Sandino)
And Nicaragua called by him
"the promised land of world communism"
Every encounter with another is with the Other.
Although it's dangerous to speak of God
says Origen.

Galileo found the system very complicated;
with the earth not in the center
it was simplified.
      The third planet.
Where solar radiation made us see.
Without us the universe is blind.
(although planetary means the same as infinitesimal)
Those who don't believe that we will be better

and those who do.
And Reeves says:
                    Man was born of the primate
                    what will be born of man?
          Those who call Utopia utopian.
It was once. Not any more with the present technology.
That night with Fidel in the University.
A huge round table with the students. Fidel said:
"Socialism is anti-instinct.
Capitalism is very dangerous because it's very attractive.
Socialism is at a disadvantage because it's sacrifice."

There are no traces of feces
of extraterrestrials on the Earth.
Could this part of the Galaxy be uninhabited?
Or do they not exist and we're alone in the universe?
Or are they trying to communicate, like us?
Or are they studying us?
                    The so-called "Mediocrity Principle":
A planet and a sun are pretty routine.

          Like a small baby in its mother's arms.
"We're all children of the same Mother"
was Aleksandr Aleksandrov's message
when he saw the USA and USSR under snow.

Maybe one day there'll be a spherical city:
          The entire earth.

Sin is going against evolution.
The irruption of the future in the present
that's evolution.
The future which is forever arriving
and sweeps the present into the past.
Evolution is revolutions.
                    "Changes in the species
                    are not continuous but discontinuous"
We've already seen it had a beginning

how will it end?
Black holes which are a mass without matter,
where physics comes to an end
and theory of Relativity no longer obtains?
  With a firm step entering the black future . . .
Solar system after solar system, galaxy after galaxy
will be extinguished.
According to Relativity
everything is relative except the speed of light.
  Among the black holes of nevermore.
And light always takes the shortest route.
Every being tends to transcend itself, and that's Evolution.
There are dolphins that have almost spoken English,
in underwater acoustics which is sometimes ultrasonic.
Their sonar and radar are better than ours.
In non-anthropocentric technology a high technology.
Their brain more convoluted than ours.
Their underwater vision is the same as in the air
and on the surface half aerial and half aquatic vision.
  —We don't know their intelligence

  Every being tends to transcend itself.
  To be superior to the being before.
  So won't human beings tend too
  to transcend into another better being?
  But it's dangerous to speak of God.

We are animals, which are chemical elements, which
are atoms, which are just a haze of probabilities.
So how can chance be the cause of order? Talbot says
that electrons appear to make decisions.
And Dyson: "The mind is inherent to the electron."
Although if life heading towards more life
violates the second law, the sacred second law
this is not the case, says Paul Davies.

There is order even in the foam of a torrent.
"Chaos" is now a technical term

which doesn't mean chaotic but a more hidden order
(formation of clouds, cyclones, New York Stock Exchange)
and we have to discover the order in the apparent chaos.

> Baseball pitched
> to some or to no applause,
> correctly or incorrectly
> which wasn't stopped in the glove
> and flew where it willed

The formula is:
All united but each one is one.
And according to Bohm
all things touch,
all connected with all
and all is instantaneous.
The separation is apparent.
This is the most important gift
of quantum physics, almost
like a science fiction story.
There are no separate particles
says Bohm.
Science fiction taken seriously.

A child on deck gazing at the stars
and sitting beside him Jose Martí.
Later, in his nineties, he recorded Martí's words
for Cintio Vitier.
"Do you think it was made for us to contemplate it
briefly? Don't you think
my boy, that there has to be something greater than us?
                    Do you realize
what it represents and that we down here
we're part of it?
Well just so as you know that it wasn't made to amuse us
and we have obligations towards what's been created."

Now Wheeler asks
what use is a universe without consciousness of that universe.

And adds that the universe is so big
because it couldn't be any other way.
And Barrow:
Our existence is the cause of the universe's structure.
        That's very mysterious physics.
That physical conditions could produce man, fine.
But that man could produce the physical conditions
so he could appear later in the future?

"The universe had to create observers of itself."

A child on deck gazing at the stars
and sitting beside him Jose Martí.

At Delphos

After the ruins and hungry by now
we stopped to lunch in a restaurant close to the highway.
        Small tables with a paper cloth
                under the laurel trees.
Nearby, a whole lamb roasted over coals.
They served us tenderloin, liver and intestines of lamb:
tomato salad, onion, goat cheese and
purple olives bruised from their ripeness,
     everything swimming in olive oil;
a yellow wine in a glass bottle
with pine resin which gave it a certain earthy taste
        and Pepsi-Cola too.
Parnassus right in front of our tables,
an ordinary mountain but split in two,
     "the biceps of Parnassus" Ovid said.
And below there's an ordinary spring:
        Castalia.
You can reach Delphos by bus now,
an ordinary bus with a sign that says *Delphos*.

Passenger in Transit in Santo Domingo

From the glass lounge of the airport to the Iberia plane
        along the grey runway
                clutching my transit passenger pass
        and a gull sweeps by.
The sea must be close, you can smell it.
        Rain was approaching.
And then clambering into the plane where I'm traveling First Class
                        to a meeting of Ministers of Culture
(the plane where they'll serve me frothy champagne the color
of urine and tasting of soap suds)
I longed for the place where the gull was heading,
some solitary cove
with coconut palms slanting over the tumbling breakers,
where I'd now be on the sand with some
yucca and fried pork, and the poet Silva, and some rum,
and which I never got to see.

Destiny of an Insect

I was in my hammock
      staring at the white wall
thinking God knows what
and suddenly a black dot on the wall
and swiftly a gleaming salamander
appeared from God knows where
                ran towards it
walking on the vertical wall as though on a flat floor
      and then there was no more black dot
            and it vanished.
I liked that.
It ate it up just as I eat
as we all eat, and as
Christ ate in joyous banquets with sinners
and he gave himself as food.
I liked it.
      Everything is food in the cosmos.
And once again nothing left but the white wall.

Cell Phone

You talk on your cell phone
and talk and talk
and laugh into your cell phone
never knowing how it was made
and much less how it works
but what does that matter
      trouble is you don't know
      just as I didn't
      that many people die in the Congo
            thousands upon thousands
            for that cellphone
            they die in the Congo
in its mountains there is coltan
            (besides gold and diamonds)
used for cell phone
condensers
            for the control of the minerals
            multinational corporations
            wage this unending war
            5 million dead in 15 years
and they don't want it to be known
                country of immense wealth
                with poverty-stricken population
80% of the world's coltan
reserves are in the Congo
the coltan has lain there for
three thousand million years
      Nokia, Motorola, Compaq, Sony
            buy the coltan
      the Pentagon too, the New York
      Times corporation too
      and they don't want it to be known
nor do they want the war to stop
so as to carry on grabbing the coltan
children of 7 to 10 years extract the coltan
            because their tiny bodies

fit into the tiny holes
for 25 cents a day
and loads of children die
due to the coltan powder
or hammering the rock
that collapses on top of them
The New York Times too
that doesn't want it to be known
and that's how it remains unknown
this organized crime
of the multinationals
the Bible identifies
truth and justice
and love and the truth
the importance of the truth then
that will set us free
also the truth about coltan
coltan inside your cell phone
on which you talk and talk
and laugh into your cell phone

Vision in Grand Canary

Immensely more complex than a star
life

                first just a cell without a nucleus
                a droplet of water within a membrane
      born out of the sea
and is now to be found by the sea in Grand Canary
bodies without clothes only the genitals covered
                the beautiful primate that we are
the beach full of sunshades and beach loungers
           in the distance colored boats
                    and an intense blue sea
          with waves the color of snow and solar light
the tall gleaming buildings
behind the barren hills—moonscape—
and further back the blue mountains
          now by night the bay is black
          and the water heavy as petroleum
            the row of hotels shimmering in it
now is the feast of the Virgin of Light
with thousands on the seafront avenue
      dancing drinking eating
      pressed up against each other
            you can hardly walk
couples standing their skins as close together as possible
          delight of skin rubbing against skin
and beneath the variegated light
like a river the procession
         of the Virgin of Light
traditional costumes and costumes
of every color contained in solar light
      they sing and laugh and applaud and cheer
this life that emerged from the sea
how this species loves
how it loves itself
         the species descended from fish
         and before the life that emerged from the sea

humanity is loving one another
our primate bodies that will rise again
      because God is of the living and not the dead
          individual salvation
          implies the salvation of all
             not just on this planet
             but throughout the universe
at dawn a Jurassic machine
      with an eye of flickering light
left the sand smooth and clean again
and this was my vision in Grand Canary
            of life that emerged from the sea.

In Malta

On the island of Malta
between Libya and Sicily
I planted an olive tree.

I remember Malta with its big ships
black hulls and white above, as
tall as the forts next to them,
the yellow-stone forts the ramparts
of which jut into the sea like prows
        rampart upon rampart
        upon rampart
    with round towers along them.
(The bay they used to close with a chain
when corsairs appeared).
           On this island of Malta, the island
           of the Knights of Malta:
the blue Mediterranean surrounding us
dashed to white on the rocks.
The same old alleyways of
yesteryear, but with tv aerials.
Wine-blue sea to the horizon
if there is a blue wine.
Its gentle gradations of blue, they say. Or
Where the blue turns to green and the green foam.
    Or:
        Rough waves
           green and white
              striped.
The shore so clear you can't see
the water, just the algae on the bottom.
Opposite Circe's island
        where Ulysses spent seven years
        there being no tourist guides then.
Upon an indigo-blue, fishing boats
with the eyes of Osiris on the prow
    (alongside luxury yachts).

It wasn't the tourist season.
The sea was cold.

      Fluorescent blue water in the grotto
      where sirens were once seen
      and one can believe they can still be seen
      when the sun is refracted pink
      and mauve by the sands on the bottom.
      but they would sing at night
      and one can believe they can still be heard
      when the night wind resounds
      loudly in the grotto.

The island where St. Paul was shipwrecked
(60 A. D.) perhaps close to our hotel.
Pastel-colored houses with flat roofs
against an arid background.
The March fields with rosy clover
and the sea glimpsed between the pines.
The island of honey and roses according to Cicero.
Almost without soil, the ground just stones, and
entirely crisscrossed with stone walls.
Teeming with cacti too that Columbus introduced.
      The tiny village below the cliffs
      with simple restaurants, and
      next to the megalithic temple
                  hot-dogs.

Very close, behind Circe's island:
in Sicily, the Pershing missiles
                      threatening.
They wouldn't let us disembark there
in peaceful protest.
Minuscule fish-shaped Malta
coveted by every empire:
Roman, Ottoman, Nelson, Napoleon, NATO
free now and at peace for the first time
since the Phoenicians. There I wrapped up

a meeting of pacifists and guerrillas
with the message:
Neither liberation without peace nor peace without liberation.
—"Justice and Peace have kissed" says the Psalm—

Free and at peace for the first time, the island
with its new socialist government,
where in the name of Nicaragua I planted an olive tree
that by now should be big, blowing in the wind
its green branches of olive green uniform
                    in protest against
                    the gringo missiles.

Visit to Germany (1973)

Tiny little houses with sharp-sloping roofs
like an endless succession of villages
                                as far as the eye can see
when the plane approaches Frankfurt.
But it's still not Frankfurt.
And when the plane begins to taxi
                rapidly the trees
red, green, orange and yellow hues,
the German autumn in all its splendor.
In the airport urinals
a small machine that sells condoms
        of a brand with "greater sensitivity"
it provokes in me the yearning for a mystical union
                (with God and the people).
I ask: Give me that greater sensitivity.

At the Frankfurt Book Fair
posters of me.
A huge photo of me with Allende.
Autographs.
Girls and boys with long hair filing by.
"Many books on Hitler this year—Hermann tells me.
It's a kind of nostalgia."
German women the color of apples.
                Apples and peaches.

Hair the color of sunlight
                or of electric light.
                        In a book on Sexuality: close-up
of the penis entering the vagina.
To me it's the photo
                (*Sacramentum*)
of the union of Christ with his Church.
At the Fair they interview me for the radio
Count Ludwig von Schonfeldt.
                An expert on Latin American literature

Count Ludwig von Schonfeldt.

Interview after interview.

The young Swiss psychiatrist, hearing me mention Somoza:

"Is it a tolerant dictatorship like the Swiss one?"

"The Swiss one?"

"Yes. It's not how you foreigners think.

They allow protest in the newspapers

as long as you don't threaten capitalism.

Peasants are peasants generation after generation.

They can never go to a university.

There are poor, although not like those in South America.

A tolerant repression . . . "

Old restaurant in Frankfurt:

Venison with mushrooms. And chilled white wine.

I'd forgotten the taste of wine in Europe.

Wines of my youth in Europe.

Not having returned to Europe in 23 years.

At my publisher's reception, in Wuppertal,

a pink-faced young man, celestial eyes, lemon-yellow hair

says to me:

"You're in the country of idealism.

Remember that Hegel was an idealist.

And those before him,

and his followers.

And idealism prevents us from seeing reality.

To us, Christianity

is ideas.

Christ is an idea,

and he is not the poor."

Wuppertal, Sunday morning,

peaceful,

no traffic.

Every window closed,

they're all sleeping.

By car along the autobahn, and suddenly in the night

clouds of smoke and infernal glows

of laboratories.
                    The whole air with a pungent smell.
Amid apple trees laden with apples
            and pruned cherry trees
                    the old XIIth century abbey
where the old abbot told me:
"This was once a castle,
                        but it's not impregnable.
There are many changes in the Church
and we don't know what's going to happen,
we are only certain of the next day.
But I think that these big changes occurring in the Church
are because the whole world is heading
for a kind of big Revolution."

We pass by a paper factory,
                Germany's biggest.
Then a forest of chimneys. This is all Krupp
poisoning the air.
But on the autobahns
                there are no commercial hoardings.
Hazy pines through the fog.
        On a grey bridge, graffiti
in white letters:
        LONG LIVE COMMUNIST GERMANY

Yellow vineyards on the banks of the Rhine.
And there on the banks of the Rhine
we enter a castle with red ramparts
                            with reddish creepers
where there is a community of young revolutionaries.
The sober lunch, salads, cold pastas,
                and dialogue with them after the coffee.
And after I've already said my farewells
            a young man comes up to me and says

almost as a secret:
"Don't imagine that all young people are like that."

The Rhine: all the chimneys smoking at the same time.
The whole valley smelling of sulfuric acid.
        Mountains of coal, trains
                carrying coal, sky
                        clouded by the coal.

Next to the railway station
        the filigree of Cologne Cathedral;
the bells of the cathedral
                amid the flurry of pigeons.
Inside, in the penumbra, Gregorian chant.
From the tower: the Rhine and the bridges;
                the factories as though on fire.
In the square a young girl breaks away from her group
and runs up to me:
"Are you Ernesto Cardenal?"
        Like a cherub in blue jeans.
A large insurance company
has been buying up houses in the old quarter
to tear them down
        and put up apartment blocks.
Bearded, ex-hippie,
                with political placard on the street.
They were changing the names of the squares
                to those of Allende and Neruda.
Heinrich Böll, a Catholic,
tells me in his Cologne apartment:
"The German Catholic Church is the worst in the world.
More backward than the Spanish Church.
                More even than the Irish Church."
Taking tea and cognac with him and his wife
in his apartment, where he never answers the phone.

Close to Cologne
                we go by La Bayer.

Poisoned sky.
Then a huge plastics factory
                shrouded in smoke.

The fields of Westphalia,
Maize, young wheat, Holstein cows and old oak trees.
"The peasants here—Peter tells me—
for centuries were vassals of the bishop of Münster
and for this reason they're conservative."
And Hermann told me:
"I think to young people Peter is now the best German musician."
In Peter's backyard I cut green juicy apples.
Then a fire was lit in the hearth;
                above it, handicrafts from Solentiname.
In the house of a peasant from Westphalia:
fine curtains,
        pictures, vases, modern lamps.
By the fireside he offers us a brandy from Avignon.
"Why are the Nicaraguan peasants so poor?"
he asks me. Because we'd spoken about Solentiname.
                But his son cannot go to the university.
A religious service in Münster with around 1000 young people,
        and music from Peter.
                In the prayer,
asking pardon for having exploited poor countries,
        blond heads bowed.
Peter whispers in my ear:
"Before, young people like these were followers of Hitler."

In the sacristy of Münster Cathedral
        the coffer where the bishop kept the money
                (enormous coffer)
                        taken from the peasants.
Up above, hanging from the tower some iron cages
from centuries gone by,
        with the skeletons of heretics

(Anabaptist communists)
that were eaten there by the birds.

Close to Peter's house
                a company that sells earth:
They sell earth in plastic bags
         in huge quantities, to all cities.
(Speaking of the two Germanys):
"In East Germany—one says
they can believe literally in all the commercial advertising
from the West, that they see on television:
that the washing powder leaves clothes white as snow, for example,
which housewives here know not to be true
but they have no way of proving it."
        A young man asks me if I like Germany
and I say yes. He says to me:
        "We're a colony of the United States."
And the boy from Hanover
        with curls and a split-beard
like the conventional image of Christ
who had refused to enter the army.
        And a Protestant parish
that sent money to the guerillas in Angola.

In Wuppertal, the city of Engels,
Dieter Rosenkranz, a millionaire like Engels
and owner of textile factories in several countries
wants socialism so they'll take away his factories.
He's not interested in money.
                He takes left-wingers to his textile plants
so they can criticize them,
they tell him what else he can do for the workers.
While we have dinner in his simple house, full of great paintings,
he tells me of his visit to the Dalai Lama.
            Interested in contemplation
        and in the revolution.

And while I was speaking in an auditorium in Wuppertal
an old bearded Nazi kept

interrupting me.

    (A maniac, they explained to me.)

The two brothers descendents of Engels
in their eighties, Protestant pastors
and both important theologians.
    Moselle wine mild as lemonade
        chilled and golden, and peach pastries.
Out the windows the old and sloping roofs of Wuppertal
in the autumn afternoon, and the park.
Engels's grandfather, a merchant, went broke
at the time of Napoleon,
and showed his ledgers to the workers
so they could see he wasn't fooling them.
Once a worker stole some coal
and he delivered a cartful of coal to his house.
Friedrich's father had 50 houses.
    And there's a poem by Engels
written before his confirmation
that says: "Christ, how I love you."
But he saw the exploitation of the workers
    and he abandoned Christianity.

Marx freely chose the poor
out of love for the poor.—And the persecutions.
    Engels the same.
"I hope to meet him in heaven,"
the older of the two tells me,
in his wheelchair, with a paralyzed hand.
And when I spoke to him of life after death,
in which I believe,
        his wife
           hid her tears.

Rally in Grenada

Blue sea, bluer in parts,
       greenish (in patches) then greener still.
Some large rocks with waves breaking
          —white upon the blue—
The sky is pale against the intense blue sea.
Tiny white triangles in the blue.
      White church against the sea blue.
       A postcard of an island.
The English and French houses told apart by their roofs.
This island changed hands like a tennis ball.
        Coconut and palm trees.
         The tropical almond with horizontal branches,
and *chilamates* which are trees with roots on their branches.
You see nutmeg and cinnamon among the lianas.
       Poor houses between bougainvilleas.
Here humanity is the color of earth.
Coffee earth, and damp black earth
      humid humus.
Ferns, plantains, round and colored leaves.
Plants of Rousseau Le Douanier line the road.
Fleshy cacti. We saw from a bridge
     bare-breasted women washing clothes.
Revolutionary slogans among the flame trees and the breadfruit.
      The gentle perfume of the frangipani.
Plants my grandmother's gardener grew
             here grow wild.
There are no poisonous snakes on this island.
Every shade of green silhouetted against the greens.
A dark girl, in her orange hand a red almond.
Small white houses amid the green.
The boats crisply white against the blue.
In English it's pronounced *Grenayda.*
Little black girl in shorts like a tropical fruit.
The skin of her legs appears to smile at us.
     —Her entire skin like smiling black lips.
Columbus knew this island.

A huge rally close to the sea.
Green of the vegetation and olive green of the uniforms.
You see
the beauty of nature and the beauty of the Revolution.
The ovation for Bishop echoes
across the whole of St. George's Bay.
You see golden sands, silvery further off and turquoise sea.
A black woman eating a yellow mango in the crowd.
They applaud swaying their bodies, dancing.
Strings of paper pennants fluttering in the sky, in the distance
a patch of blue-pink sea.
Black adolescent with red sweater and breasts large as coconuts.
Rally of variegated colors like fruit and flowers.
An island of 120 square miles and 110 thousand inhabitants
(its militia of 350 with uniforms donated by Nicaragua)
a tiny island in the middle of the ocean
standing up to the United States.

Tourist in Ararat

Ararat where Noah's ark came to rest.
       It was in the USSR,
two and a half hours outside Moscow, by Aeroflot:
       Arriving at the ultra-modern airport
of millenary Armenia, I saw
a snowcapped mountain above the clouds, like another cloud
       with its intangible ark

                          Ararat.

Which infuriated a Tsar
because it couldn't be seen even once
when he was here.
       Then in the city, above
the rectilinear housing blocks and hotels,
       once again, snow amid the clouds:
                         Ararat.

The eyes of the Virgin of the sanctuary
same as those of the girl in the museum.

Vines and rosebushes along the highway
that bordered the valley of Ararat
and in the car eating Noah's grapes
like slender female fingers.

A hunched old lady in the dark crypt
gestures to request a light, and with my lighter
I light her candle for the tomb of a long-lost saint.
Hunched even more,
            she kisses the fringe of the altar cloth.

Like gigantic amphorae in the distance,
the atomic center.
       5 amphorae. One smoking.
Above which, towering in the sky,

                              Ararat.
Where 1000 of Hadrian's soldiers became anchorites.

It's been said that the Earthly Paradise was in Armenia.
          At least the Tigris and the Euphrates are here . . .
(I also read once
that the most beautiful women in the world are from here).

In front of the Greco-Roman temple
a pear tree with pears still green
and under the pear tree
          another girl again with the eyes of the icon:
large black eyes with thick joined eyebrows.

The main production is electrical instruments
          and the wine that Xenophon drank,
as told in *Anabasis,*
and which is now the USSR's famous cognac.

Its chili in traditional dishes
                    —such as *khorovats,* Caucasian kebab—
                                        the same as jalapeño
Which comes from which?
          Maize naturally comes from America.
A whole field of it extends to the horizon, and in it
the high tension pylons of the atomic center.

Large eyes and long lashes and thick eyebrows . . .

          And the apricot that originates from here
and that Alexander the Great . . . But there are two apricot faces
I remember: the old lady, and her two grandchildren with apricot
                                                  faces
the three arguing with a factory worker from Moscow
who ranted furiously that God does not exist.

"Or he let two million Armenians be massacred!"
(in front of the gigantic memorial to the Armenian martyrs).
"A God unable to do everything is possible" I butted in.
And he grew madder.

Then the boy from India, head shaved,
who came here to study for the priesthood,

to the USSR.
He's not a revolutionary, he told me, nor not a revolutionary
because in Calcutta there is no revolution.
(Ever-ready his seminarist novice smile).

Next to a cuneiform inscription
a computer factory.

Archaic

Soviet Socialist Republic.
That the ark came to rest here
is a time-honored Armenian tradition.

Reflections of a Minister

What can you do. I'm the Minister of Culture,
heading for a reception in some such embassy.
Which one? Why say the name?
This one or that, it's all the same.
And suddenly by the sidewalk, in the undergrowth
                    a cat.
The car's two lights latch onto the cat's two.
I'd like to stay there
            take a better look at this cat,
                    what color is it,
(at night they're all the same so they say)
            what would be its next move, how
would it arch its back.
To stay by the road side with the cat
                            my cat
would be better
            albeit in imitation of Marianne Moore
—that cat of hers for example mouse in its mouth
tail dangling like a shoe lace—.
Of Marianne Moore Davenport says:
"She's more intrigued by the ostrich
            than the ornithologist
                    who contributed *Ostrich*
to the Encyclopedia Britannica."
There I am thinking of the cat and Marianne Moore.
                No more:
I've now entered the brightly lit embassy
                and I greet Mr. Ambassador.

The Eagle

I saw the Bald Eagle, the American Eagle,
in the heart of Oregon. Immense prairies of sage grass
that only the buffalo can digest, not cattle,
Which is why they are deserted.
                              Neither buffalo nor Indians.
        In the distance the mesas as though machine-cut.
In the rickety pickup with Alberto, an ornithologist,
we watched as it attacked a Peregrine in flight
that dropped what it was carrying, "maybe mouse or something."
Down it swooped to where the food had fallen.
Looking from side to side, its breast puffed out, shoulders hunched,
sharp profile, ferocious
                just as it is on the coin,
and rapidly it flew off with what it had stolen from the poor Peregrine.
        The American Eagle

Snap of Segovia

          Segovia is pink in color: pink
roof tiles and bricks and towers and Roman apses
upon which the towering creamy pink cathedral stands out
but the king and queen's castle is rather a creamy yellow
        and it ends abruptly, cut sharply
        like the keel of a ship below
        which there is the abyss.
The Roman aqueduct is grey naturally
arch upon arch of stone still carrying water
where the city sinks into a hollow.
All the rest a mass of pink houses.
        Dark green
                    cypresses all round
on the billiard green baize of the meadows
where there are yellowish sheep grazing
beneath a drizzle of transparent needles.

European Postcards

Behind the floral iron balconies,

                         the pink sea.

Striped awnings and colored sunshades,
and the voices of girls on the tennis court

                         under the laurels.

Or the balcony where the girl hangs her stockings.
Stockings amid carnations. A cage of canaries.
Red roofs with moss, and beyond, the sea. Below
the alleyway
smelling of fried sardines, the cry
of the oyster seller,

                         and a gramophone.

White hotels bordering the bay.
Prussian blue sea beneath cobalt sky.
Nets strung out to dry fragrant algae,
and the old men mending the nets.
And there is a tower there between the oaks,
and three turrets in ruins on some rocks.
The promenade under the lime trees, close to the moat.
The castle of yellow bricks.

Hills and yellow ramparts above them,
the shadows of the clouds above the olive groves,
and the singing of the women harvesting olives.

Or there is a round tower:
Stone covered in ivy.   Blue sea
beyond the battlements

                     A sail
on the sea.

             Flight of white gulls.

A cart goes by laden with girls
along the road bordered by flowering chestnuts.
And the smell of the chestnut flower.

The whistle of a shepherd boy in the distance. Sound
of a horn.
A golden flock where the sun is setting.

A tower reflected in the river:
and they are identical the real and the unreal.

An ethereal smoke rises in the village
                    to the sound of a flute.
There is a muddy plough abandoned in a field
                    (and a song with flute).

Smoke, grimy gulls, the ships'
horns,
the cranes and the masts under a leaden sky,
leaden smoke and smell of ozone,
the cry of itinerant vendors,
and a *fado* . . .
                    And the smell of the salty night.
The distant lights of the hotels and the cinemas.
Palaces reflected in the putrid water.
The black gondolas with black gondoliers.
Thick cables, oily water, a barrel on the wharf.
The grey ship of the USA Navy.
And the night waters lapping the steps
or splashing beneath the launches
and the launches bumping against the wharf
or launch bumping against launch.
The lagoon lit by red and green lights,
and the light of a gondola, and the sound of the oar . . .

On the Banks of the Ohio in Kentucky

Kentucky is a second paradise, said Daniel Boone.
He went in search of Kentucky traveling out west,
and from a hilltop he saw the plains of Kentucky,
the buffalo grazing as on cattle farms
and the silent Ohio through the broad flatlands
bordering Kentucky . . .

(and which now smells of phenol).

Forest Grove Prairie Village Park Forest Deer Park
              frontier names!
are now the names of suburban condominiums.

Buses cross the prairies where the buffalo roamed.

Where the pioneer of the frontier once camped
as he migrated in a canoe towards the Missouri river
with his carbine and tomahawk and his beaver traps,
following the beavers
the sound of lawnmowers now resounds,
the tinkle of highballs, laughter, the raucous radio,
shouts from the games of croquet and volleyball
and the dull thud of the baseball in the glove.
From an open window a hi-fi blares
and, with the smell of barbecued meats, wafts in the night.

All was still . . .

—writes Daniel Boone—

I lit a fire by a spring
To roast the loin of a deer I'd killed.
The wolves howled all night long . . .

And now all the sewers spew industrial waste,
chemical substances into the Ohio.
Household detergents have killed the fish
and the Ohio smells of phenol . . .

Traveling on a Bus through the United States

Many years ago from a bus in Virginia or Alabama
I saw
a pink girl, in blue pants
standing on a ladder, picking apples
(her mother calling her from inside)
and another girl, her sister, blue pants
painting the porch of the house white
            —And they gazed at the bus as it went by and accelerated.
Time has gone by like the Greyhound bus
but they've remained, despite the years, the paint
fresh on the porch
                the brush dripping
the hand on the apple, their gazes
many years ago, one morning, Virginia or Alabama
           forget which state.

The Place Called "Harmony"

He was traveling slowly in case he got there too early
and she was traveling fast because she was going to be late.

He was traveling along one highway and she along another
and the two cars collided at the intersection
of the two highways (the place called "Harmony").

The police said the probability of an accident was
"a million to one,"
because the two highways were very wide at that spot
and the drivers of the two vehicles
had to have seen each other perfectly
"unless the two of them had been distracted
thinking about the place they were both heading . . ."

But the police didn't know that he and she had made a date
and that the two cars that collided were heading for the same place.
The coincidence was greater than the police knew:
Neither one in a million nor one in a billion
but one in an infinity of probabilities
or rather there was no coincidence or probability
and what happened couldn't have been any other way:
he and she had made a date
and they'd synchronized their watches
and they were too punctual on the date.

That is all.

Apalka

Only in summer, in the brief summer, is it accessible.
Descending the river Coco from the last Miskito settlement
downstream about five marine miles to the left
a narrow river emerges called the Caño de Apalka.
If you ascend this river they say you reach a lagoon
     and then another lagoon
and then the mysterious lagoon of Apalka.
(You arrive at an endless plain, full of colors
orchids and toucans, like in the cinema or in some dream
     and in the middle of this plain: a lagoon.)
Voices apparently of people are heard on its edges
and right in the center of the deep waters.
According to what the oldest Indians tell
who heard the elders of their tribe tell
many many years ago
pirates ascended the Patuca river
and entered via a secret stream to the final lagoon
     to divide their booty in this hideaway
and they fought over the booty and all perished.
You can still see, or can maybe see, the masts and rigging
     tangled beneath lianas and reeds
and between rotten trunks, indistinguishable from the trunks
the rotten hulls, a jumble, surrounded by water lilies.
The Indians of the Coco never venture into the mysterious lagoon
afraid of the voices that are heard on its edges,
since the spirits of the dastardly souls still watch over the booty
     and are fighting still
and you hear the cries (like toucans) and gunshots
and at night you hear the dragging of chains, like raising anchors.
     Sometimes the thrash of an alligator
          fighting with another alligator . . .
The occasional fin cutting the calm waters of the lagoon:
a shark that entered like the pirates through the Pituca
or perhaps a swordfish.
When the wet season arrives the Apalka lagoon is no more
     and the plain is no more

there's just a lake as far as the horizon
obliterated the place where the Apalka lagoon exists
with galleons laden with silver and gold and pearls
and the skeletons of pirates
        everything, skeletons and treasure, sunken in the mud.
But maybe there's a moon, and the infinite lagoon
that no one from the Coco visits
becomes (on the wind the irate voices of pirates)
by the light of the moon of the Atlantic night, a
        lugubrious lagoon of silver coins.

Notes

Source for the Foreword

Anne Waldman, "Revolution/Evolution, an interview with Ernesto Cardenal," in *Outrider* (Albuquerque, NM: La Alameda Press, 2006).

Notes for the Introduction

1. In addition to the title poem, *The Origin of Species and Other Poems* includes nineteen new poems, the majority of which have never been published previously and none of which is available in book form in English. However, the poems have been arranged so that Cardenal's most recent production appears first, followed by thirteen poems from earlier phases in his career (some of which are also appearing for the first time in English translation). This approach is intended to underscore the consistency of Cardenal's method of composition over time, or as he recently wrote to me: "en mi poesía no hay diferencias cronológicas" ("there are no chronological differences in my poetry").

2. In the recapitulation and conclusion to *The Origin of Species*, originally published in 1859, Darwin wrote: "Analogy would lead me one step further, namely, to the belief that all animals and plants have descended from some one prototype." Notice how Cardenal uses the power of poetry to dramatically crystallize Darwin's critical observation.

3. Published in 1905 in *Cantos de vida y esperanza* (*Songs of Life and Hope*), the opening two lines of Darío's poem read: "It would take the voice of the Bible, or the verse of Walt Whitman / to reach you, O Hunter."

4. Whitman is widely regarded as the founding father of modern North American poetry and an influence on Rubén Darío, who, as leader of the *Modernista* movement, is credited as being the founder of modern Hispanic poetry. Cardenal's equally innovative poetics embraces the legacy of both cultures.

5. Quotations from Whitman's "Song of Myself," sections 24 and 31 respectively, originally published in 1855.

6. Published as *Love*, Ernesto Cardenal (London: Search Press, 1974).

7. *The Poems of Marianne Moore*, Grace Schulman, ed. (New York: Viking, 2003).

About the Author

The author of more than thirty-five books, many translated into multiple languages, Nicaraguan poet **Ernesto Cardenal** was ordained as a Roman Catholic priest in 1965. His studies with Trappist monk Thomas Merton and his involvement with the Sandinista movement in his home country have informed his writing and political activism. He lives in Managua, Nicaragua, where he is vice president of Casa de los Tres Mundos, a literary and cultural organization.